RENÉ DAUMAL AND ROGER GILBERT-LECOMTE

a bibliography

PHIL POWRIE

Grant & Cutler Ltd
1988

© Grant & Cutler Ltd
1988
ISBN 0 7293 0302 0

333477

�'𝒞

I.S.B.N. 84-599-2557-9

DEPÓSITO LEGAL: V. 2.821 - 1988

Printed in Spain by Artes Gráficas Soler, S.A., Valencia

for

GRANT & CUTLER LTD
55-57 GREAT MARLBOROUGH STREET, LONDON W1V 2AY

RESEARCH BIBLIOGRAPHIES & CHECKLISTS

48

René Daumal and Roger Gilbert-Lecomte:
a bibliography

RESEARCH BIBLIOGRAPHIES & CHECKLISTS

RₑB

General editors

A.D. Deyermond, J.R. Little and J.E. Varey

AUM MAHA SHIVA NAMAH

Contents

INTRODUCTION

The aim of this bibliography is to provide students of René Daumal and Roger Gilbert-Lecomte with a record of their writings and criticism relating to it. A 'double' bibliography seemed appropriate given their frequent collaboration and the recent resurgence of interest in the periodical they masterminded, *Le Grand Jeu*.

The principle I have adopted is one of inclusiveness; I have given as much information as possible, with the following exceptions. I have excluded anthologies published after the authors' deaths; and I have not provided book sizes. My argument for including the usually excluded histories of literature and ephemeral newspaper reviews is that they are important, if crude, barometers of literary taste. *Le Grand Jeu* has suffered from its associations with Surrealism, which have tended to blur substantial differences. The evolution of critical taxonomies is thus of crucial importance.

The bibliography is in two sections, Primary Material, and Secondary Material. Both are organised chronologically in units of one year. In the first section, Primary Material, there are two sub-sections in each year unit, the first devoted to the writings of Daumal, the second to those of Gilbert-Lecomte. Each sub-section lists works in separate chronological order although the item codes run in numerical sequence through both sub-sections.

Entry codes

For Primary Material:

Aa Books and pamphlets.
Ab Articles, poems, reviews and prefaces published in periodicals, and collective declarations written by the author.
Ac Articles or declarations written in collaboration with others, and declarations signed, but not written, by the author.
Ae Works translated from the English by Daumal.

As   Works translated from the Sanskrit by Daumal.
At   Translations of works by Daumal or Gilbert-Lecomte into other languages.

For Secondary Material:

Ba   Books, theses and numbers of periodicals the whole or a substantial part of which are devoted to Daumal, Gilbert-Lecomte, or Le Grand Jeu.
Bb   Articles, reviews, parts of books or theses devoted to the above. These also include ephemeral newspaper reviews, except in cases where the book is no more than mentioned.

The general presentation should not present any problems. Items are entered under their original title wherever possible. There are five exceptions: letters, unless published under a title, are entered under a standard form, 'Letter to [Surname], [Christian name], dated [date]'. In the case of a collection of letters in one volume, only the name of the addressee and the date are entered after the indication 'Letters to...'; in the case of a collection of letters in one volume to a single addressee only the date is entered after the indication 'Letters to [Christian name], [Surname]'. The second exception to entry under original title is in the case of items which could lead to confusion; thus, for example, Gilbert-Lecomte's two 'Rêve de mort' are entered with their first words in square brackets so as to distinguish them for the purposes of cross-referencing and indexing. The third exception is in the case of texts by Gilbert-Lecomte generally. Many of his works were originally untitled fragments; they have been entered under the title ascribed to them by the first editor. The fourth exception is in As items by Daumal, where a key-word from the original Sanskrit title is given in square brackets if it is not already in the title. The fifth exception is in Ae items by Daumal, where the English title is given in square brackets in addition to the French title.

Place of publication is Paris unless otherwise specified. Book items give the details as found on the cover or title page. Periodical items have the volume number, if it is available, in Roman numerals, the issue number in Arabic numerals, followed by the place of publication (in cases other than Paris), and the date in parentheses. Dates and places of publication (with the exception of 'Saigon') are given in the language of the country of publication. Dates are abbreviated on the lines '15 jan. 1945' for '15 janvier 1945'. An asterisk before the item indicates that I have not seen the item personally. A few items have no more than the most basic information; these are items which I have consulted in files of press-cuttings and which I have not been able to trace back to more detailed sources.

Introduction

Items found in one location, whether this be an issue of a periodical, or a collected edition, are listed as decimal entries, unless they require a different entry code from the main item. This occurs, for example, in the case of an item which contains poems and articles requiring an Ab code, and texts in collaboration requiring an Ac code. The latter are itemised separately, unless they are reprints, in which case the entry code is determined by any new item.

Chronology

Entries are in strict chronological order according to the most precise dating available from the publication. In the case of periodicals it is assumed that monthly periodicals appear on the first of the month unless otherwise stated. For periodicals with seasonal dates of publication I have adopted the following procedure:

Spring   : 1 March
Summer   : 1 June
Autumn   : 1 September
Winter   : 1 December

For periodicals with trimestrial dates of publication, I have adopted the following procedure:

Trimester 1   : 1 January
Trimester 2   : 1 April
Trimester 3   : 1 July
Trimester 4   : 1 October

Periodicals or books which have no indication other than the year are placed at the end of each year unit. Periodicals whose date of publication spans two years are classed according to the first year. Wherever possible, the *achevé d'imprimer* is used to determine an otherwise less precise date; it is used systematically to determine the date of publication of books, whose copyright is also given if it is at variance with the *achevé d'imprimer*. Where two or more items occur on the same date, they are classified alphabetically, by periodical title or book title.

Pagination

Pagination lists numbered pages and all blank pages at the end of a book. Where an item is part of a book, the pagination of the item is preceded by the pagination of the book in the brackets which include other details for the book.

11

Reprints

The first occurrence of a text also lists reprints in whatever form. I have listed all reprints which have come to my notice. These give appropriate details; in the case of a book, for example, the item will specify whether the reprint is a re-edition or a new edition. Only substantial extracts which postdate the publication of the whole text are given.

The extreme fragmentation of Gilbert-Lecomte's work has necessitated more detailed cross-referencing. The first occurrence of a text is cross-referenced in the usual way, listing all reprints, but may also have a page-reference in square brackets to the standard *Œuvres complètes,* Volume I, when the fragment is difficult to locate.

Abbreviations

Apart from abbreviated dates (see above), the following abbreviations are used throughout:

RD	: René Daumal
RGL	: Roger Gilbert-Lecomte
Le GJ	: Le Grand Jeu
CR	: Critical review or 'compte rendu'

(These four will be found in square brackets after many Secondary Material items indicating the purpose or thrust of a text where this is not clear from the title. It should also be noted that items for book reviews without a specific title begin with the periodical title.)

Abr.	: Abridged
Anon.	: Anonymous
Attr.	: Attributed
CdS	: *Cahiers du Sud* [Marseille]
Ch.	: Chapter
Coll.	: Collection
Ed.	: Edited by
FMS	: Facsimile manuscript
No.	: 'Numéro'
No.sp.	: 'Numéro spécial'
NRF	: *Nouvelle Revue Française*
p.	: page
pp.	: pages
Refs	: References

Repr.   : Reprinted
Trim.   : Trimestre
Unpag. : Unpaginated
Vol.   : Volume

Indexes

There are nine indexes for Primary Material:

Index 1 : Aa items by Daumal
Index 2 : Ab and Ac items by Daumal
Index 3 : Ae items by Daumal
Index 4 : As items by Daumal
Index 5 : At items by Daumal
Index 6 : Aa items by Gilbert-Lecomte
Index 7 : Ab and Ac items by Gilbert-Lecomte
Index 8 : At items by Gilbert-Lecomte
Index 9 : Selective Index of Proper Names

Items are indexed by the title under which they are listed in the bibliography, with the following exceptions. *Letters* are listed under a standard form ('Letter to [Surname], [Christian name], [date]') even when they are listed under a French title. Postcards and telegrams are also listed under this standard form, with an indication of their nature in square brackets. Since many of the letters are undated by their authors I have wherever possible supplied the editor's dating in square brackets; this may sometimes be the date of the postmark. The *Ae index* lists texts translated by Daumal under their original English title. The *As index* lists Daumal's translations from the Sanskrit under key Sanskrit words, either titles of books or names of authors, with Daumal's spelling. The *At indexes* list items translated into other languages under the original French title. The *Selective Index of Proper Names* contains names of authors, artists, collaborators, translators and illustrators. It excludes secondary material authors, addressees of letters in the Primary Material, publishers and places of publication, and editors of texts or special numbers.

The indexes are cross-referenced, so that all reprints of an individual work are listed with their item codes.

There are two indexes for the Secondary Material:

Index 1 : Ba items
Index 2 : Bb items

Each index contains an alphabetical list of authors, also cross-referenced, so that codes for all items by an author are given under his or her name. Issues of periodicals the whole or a substantial part of which are devoted to Daumal, Gilbert-Lecomte or Le Grand Jeu are listed in the Ba index under the rubric '[Collection]' followed by the title of the periodical.

I would like to thank the following for their help: the University of Newcastle upon Tyne, for a grant which allowed me to research in France; Robert Firth and the staff of the University of Newcastle upon Tyne Library Interlibrary Loans Service, who responded positively to the most ludicrous requests; Messrs Gallimard, Jean-Michel Place, and Pierre Belfond for allowing me to consult their files of press-cuttings; Bruno and Marie-Jo Roy of Fata Morgana (Montpellier), for their kind hospitality and for allowing me to research in their library; H. Josèphe Maxwell of the Fonds Daumal (Paris), Michel Random (Paris), Alain Tourneux (Conservateur en Chef des Musées Charleville-Mézières), Viviane Couillard (Bordeaux), Monique Faux (Paris), David Thomas (Taylor Institution Library, Oxford), Ales Chalupa of the Archiv Narodniho Muzea (Prague), and Antoine Coron of the Bibliothèque Nationale (Paris) for a number of precious bibliographical details.

I am most indebted to the following: Roger Little, for his help and advice, and Juliet Horsley, for her support. My greatest debt is to Judith Hunter of the University of Newcastle upon Tyne Computing Department, without whose unfailing optimism as my Textform adviser I would not have been able to complete this project.

Department of French Studies, School of Modern Languages, The University of Newcastle upon Tyne, September 1988.

PRIMARY MATERIAL

1923

ROGER GILBERT-LECOMTE

Ab1   'Les Souvenances', *Le Pampre* [Reims], 7-8 (fév. 1923), 15.
RGL credited as Roger Lecomte. With an introduction by René
Maublanc (see Bb1). Repr. Aa319.

Ab2   Texts under title '8 haïkaï inédits' [*sic*] in *Le Pampre* [Reims],
10-11, no.sp. 'Le Haïkaï français' (26 oct. 1926).
RGL credited as Roger Lecomte.
   .1 'La branche des marronniers...', 30. Dated juill. 1923. Repr.
   Aa316, Aa319.
   .2 'Tous ces verts marronniers pansus...', 33. Dated avr. 1923.
   Repr. Aa316, Aa319.
   .3 'Le vent d'automne...', 35. Dated juill. 1923. Repr. Aa316,
   Aa319.
   .4 'La nuit...', 36. Dated jan. 1923. Repr. Aa316, Aa319.
   .5 'L'étoile pique...', 37. Dated juill. 1923. Repr. Aa316, Aa319.
   .6 'Vie d'un instant...', 37. Dated jan. 1923. Repr. Aa316,
   Aa319.
   .7 'Dans le ciel de cendre...', 38. Dated avr. 1923. Repr. Aa316,
   Aa319.
   .8 'Brouillard sur la mer', 44. Dated juill. 1923. Repr. Aa316,
   Aa319.
   .9 'La cathédrale dans les brumes...', 50. Dated jan. 1923. Repr.
   Aa316, Aa319.

1928

RENE DAUMAL

*Ab3   'La Tête et le trou', in programme for the Ursulines, soirée of 18
Feb. 1928. Repr. Ab29, Aa193, At239, Aa271.

Ac4   'Le Grand Jeu', prospectus [1928] signed 'La Direction';
      probably in collaboration with RGL. Repr. At32, Ab242, Ab254,
      Ab269, Aa288, Ab324, Ab335.

Ac5   'Avant-propos', *Le Grand Jeu*, 1 (été [18 juin] 1928), 1-3.
      Written by RGL; RD is a co-signatory. Repr. At32, At239, Ab242,
      Ab254, Ab269, Ac297, Ab308, At309, Ab324, Ab335, At347.

Ab6   Texts, ibid.
      .1 'Liberté sans espoir', 19-25. Repr. At32, At239, Ab242 (abr.),
         Ab254, Ab269, Aa288, Ab308, Ab324, At347.
      .2 'Entrée des larves', 41. Repr. Ab29, Aa193, At239, Ab254,
         Aa271, Ab308.
      .3 'Lévy-Bruhl: *L'Ame primitive*', 48-49. Repr. Aa184, Ab254,
         Aa288, Ab308.
      .4 'Jean Prévost: *Essai sur l'introspection*', 61-62. Repr. Aa184,
         Ab254, Aa288, Ab308.

Ab7   '*Le Bourreau du Pérou*, par G. Ribemont-Dessaignes', *CdS*, V, 104
      (août-sept. 1928), 148-49.

Ab8   'Poèmes', in *CdS*, V, 105 (oct. 1928), 175-76.
      .1 'A perdre sens', 175. Repr. Aa193, Aa271.
      .2 'Feu aux artifices', 176. Repr. Aa193, Aa271.

Ab9   '*Nadja*, par A. Breton', *CdS*, V, 106 (nov. 1928), 317-21. Repr.
      Ab254, Aa288.

ROGER GILBERT-LECOMTE

Ac10 'Le Grand Jeu', prospectus [1928] signed 'La Direction'; probably
      in collaboration with RD.
      Repr. At38, Ab246, Ab256, Ab275, Ab291, Ab328, Ab339.

Ab11 'Avant-propos', *Le Grand Jeu*, 1 (été [18 juin] 1928), 1-3. Written
      by RGL; RD is a co-signatory.
      Repr. At38, At245, Ab246, Ab256, Ab275, Aa301, Ab317, At318,
      Ab328, Ab339, At352.

Ab12 Texts, ibid.
      .1 'La Force des renoncements', 12-18. Repr. At38, Ab167,
         At245, Ab256, Ab275, Aa301, Ab317, At352.
      .2 '*La Crise du monde moderne*, René Guénon', 52. Repr.
         Ab256, Aa301, Ab317.
      .3 'Puériculture. L'Enfant-sage', 54-55. Repr. Ab256, Aa301,
         Ab317.

1929

RENE DAUMAL

Ab13   '*Vulturne*, par L.-P. Fargue', *CdS*, VI, 111 (avr. 1929), 227-29.
Repr. Aa184, Aa288.

Ab14   Texts in *Le Grand Jeu*, 2 (printemps [mai] 1929).
.1 'Enquête', 4. Repr. Ab20, Ab33, Ab254, Aa288, Ab308.
.2 'André Masson, Métamorphose', 32[c-d]. Note appended to
the photo of a sculpture by A. Masson. Repr. Ab242, Ab254,
Ab308.
The following four entries are in the section entitled 'Textes':
.3 'Le Prophète', 44-45. Repr. Aa193, At239, Ab254, Aa271,
Ab308.
.4 'Rires jaunes', 45. Repr. Aa193, At239, Ab254, Ab308.
.5 'Jeu d'enfant', 46. Repr. Ab29, Aa193, Ab254, Aa271, Ab308.
.6 'Feux à volonté', 47-48. Repr. Ab29, Aa99, Aa193, Ab242
(abr.), Ab254, Aa271, Ab308.
Other previously unpublished texts:
.7 'Encore sur les livres de René Guénon', 73-74. Repr. Ab178
(abr.), Ab182, Aa184, Ab254, Aa288, Ab308. Extract repr.
Ab240, Ab294.
.8 'Chez Victor Hugo. *Les Tables Tournantes de Jersey*, par
Gustave Simon', 79-80. Repr. Ab254, Aa288, Ab308.

Ac15   Texts in collaboration with RGL, ibid.
.1 'Mise au point ou Casse-dogme', 1-3. Repr. At32, Ab254,
Ab269, Aa288, Ac297, Ab308, Ab324.
.2 'Introduction [to the 'Essais' on Rimbaud]', signed
"Le GJ", 9. Repr. Ab254, Ab308, Ab359.
.3 'La Critique des critiques', 65-69. Repr. Ab254, Ac297
Ab308.

Ab16   'De quelques sculptures de sauvages', *Première Exposition du
Groupe "Le Grand Jeu". Catalogue du 8-22 juin 1929* (Editions
Bonaparte, 17pp.), 11-14. Repr. At239, Aa288.

Ab17   'La Pataphysique et la révélation du rire', *Bifur*, 2 (juill. 1929),
56-68. Repr. At239, Aa288.
Draft version repr. Aa184.4, Ab269.

Ab18   'De l'attitude critique devant la Poésie', *CdS*, no.sp. 'La Poésie et
la Critique' (déc. 1929), 80-91. Repr. Aa184, Aa288, Ab359.

17

Ab19   'Dieu, m'a dit Sima...', short text in *Sima*, catalogue of the exhibition of Sima's painting 4-31 Dec. 1929 in Galerie Povolozky, 8pp. (unpag.), [2].

Ab20   Ab14.1 under title 'Une Enquête surréaliste', in *La Révolution Surréaliste*, 12 (15 déc. 1929), 52.

ROGER GILBERT-LECOMTE

Ab21   'Introduction', to *Correspondance inédite (1870-1875) d'Arthur Rimbaud* (Editions des Cahiers Libres, 25 avr. 1929, 100pp., 930 copies), 9-23.
Repr. At245, Aa283, Aa301, At305.

Ab22   Texts in *Le Grand Jeu*, 2 (printemps [mai] 1929).
        .1 'Après Rimbaud la mort des Arts', 26-32. Repr. At245, Ab256, Ab275, Aa283, Aa301, At305, Ab317, Ab362.
    The following two entries are in the section entitled 'Textes':
        .2 'Moi et Moi', 55. Repr. Ab256, Ab317, Ab319, Ab328.
        .3 'La Foire aux bœufs', 56. Repr. Ab256, Ab317, Aa319.

Ac23   Texts in collaboration with RD, ibid.
        .1 'Mise au point ou 'Casse-dogme', 1-3. Repr. At38, Ab256, Ab275, Ab291, Aa301, Ab317, Ab328.
        .2 'Introduction [to the 'Essais' on Rimbaud]', signed "Le GJ", 9. Repr. Ab256, Ab317, Ab362.
        .3 'La Critique des critiques', 65-69. Repr. Ab256, Aa301, Ab317.

Ab24   'Ce que devrait être la peinture, ce que sera Sima', *Première Exposition du Groupe "Le Grand Jeu". Catalogue du 8-22 juin 1929*, (Editions Bonaparte, 17pp.), 3-10.
Repr. At27 (abr.), Ab225, At245, Ab255, Ab275, Aa301. Draft repr. Ab339.

Ab25   'Stop mais que quand...', preface to *Sima*, catalogue of the exhibition of Sima's painting 4-31 Dec. 1929 at the Galerie Povolozky, 8pp. (unpag.), [3].
Repr. Aa301.

Ab26   'Monsieur Morphée, empoisonneur public. Mise au point du problème des stupéfiants', *Bifur*, 4 (31 déc. 1929), 166-179.
Repr. Aa237, At245, Ab262, Aa301.

At27   'Čím by mělo býti malířství čím bude Šíma'. Sections 2 & 3 of
        Ab24 translated into Czech by A. Borovičková, *Musaion* [Praha]
        (1929-1930), 169-75.

                                1930

                          RENE DAUMAL

Ab28   'La Chute', *Variétés* [Bruxelles], II, 12 (15 avr. 1930), 842-43.
        Repr. Aa193, Aa271.

Ab29   Texts in *Commerce*, 24 (été 1930), 66-98. With the indication 'Ex-
        traits d'un recueil à paraître *Le Contre-ciel*'. Contains Ab3, Ab6.2,
        Ab14.5, Ab14.6 and
        .1 'Je parle dans tous les âges', 69-70. Repr. Aa193,
            At239, Aa271.
        .2 'Civilisation', 73-74. Repr. Aa99, Aa193, At239, Aa271.
        .3 'La Cavalcade', 77-78. Repr. Aa193, Aa271.
        .4 'La Révolution en été', 79. Repr. Aa193, Aa271.
        .5 'Dicté en 1925', 80-84. Repr. Aa193, Aa271.
        .6 'La Nausée d'être', 85-87. Repr. Aa193, At239, Aa271,
            At295.
        .7 'Il suffit d'un mot', 88-89. Repr. Aa99, Aa193, At239,
            Aa271.
        .8 'La Seule', 90-93. Repr. Ab33, Aa99, Aa193, Ab201,
            At239, Ab254, Aa271, At295.
        .9 'Préliminaires', 94-95. Repr. Aa193, Aa271.

Ab30   Poems in *ReD* [*sic*: abbreviation for *Revue Devĕtsil*] [Praha], no.sp.
        'Le GJ' (ed. Karel Teige), 8 ([Summer] 1930).
        .1 'L'Errant', 246. Repr. Aa193, Aa271, At295.
        .2 'Casse-cœur', 248. Repr. Ab187, Aa193, Aa271.

Ac31   'Le Comte de Lautréamont et la justice tchécoslovaque', ibid., 240.
        Collective declaration drafted by RGL and signed by all members
        of Le GJ. Repr. Ac34, Ab269, Ac297, Ab308.

At32   Texts translated into Czech by Jindrich Horejsi, ibid.
        Contains Ac4 and Ac5 (under title 'Le GJ. Úvodní manifest'),
        Ab6.1 (under title 'Svoboda bez nadeji'), and Ac15.1 (under title
        'Rozbití dogmat. Manifest-polemika').

Ab33   Texts in *Le Grand Jeu*, 3 (automne [oct.] 1930).

                                 19

Contains Ab14.1 (followed by two answers from René Crevel and
Carlo Suarès) and
.1 'Nerval le Nyctalope', 20-31. Repr. Aa184, At239, Ab242
(abr.), Ab254, Aa288, Ab308.
The section entitled 'Textes' has the indication 'Extraits d'un
recueil à paraître aux Editions Kra, sous le titre *Le Contre-ciel*,
avec une préface de RGL.' Contains Ab29.8 and the following text:
.2 'L'Enfui tourne court', 69-70. Repr. Aa193, At239, Ab254,
Aa271, Ab308.
Other previously unpublished texts:
.3 'Lettre ouverte à André Breton sur les rapports du surréalisme
et du Grand Jeu', 76-83. Repr. Aa213.109, At239, Ab240
(abr.), Ab254, Ab269, Aa288, Ab294 (abr.), Ab308.
.4 'A propos d'un jugement inédit de Victor Cousin sur
Giordano Bruno', 88-90. Repr. Ab254, Aa288, Ab308.
.5 'Explications scientifiques', 90-91. Repr. Ab254, Ab308.

Ac34   Texts in collaboration, ibid.
Contains Ac31 (without title) and
.1 Collective declaration on Roger Vailland's withdrawal from
Le GJ, 2. Signed RD [*sic*], RGL[*sic*], and R[oger] V[ailland].
Repr. Ab254, Ab308, Ab363.

Ab35   'Le Comte de Lautréamont et la critique', *NRF*, XXXV, 206
(1 nov. 1930), 738-45. Repr. Ab277, Aa288.

ROGER GILBERT-LECOMTE

Ab36   'Ce que voit et ce que fait voir Sima aujourd'hui', *Documents*, 5
([2e trim.] 1930), 301-02. Repr. Aa301.

Ab37   'Le Comte de Lautréamont et la justice tchécoslovaque', *ReD* [*sic*:
abbreviation for *Revue Devĕtsil*] [Praha], no.sp. 'Le GJ' (ed. Karel
Teige), 8 ([Summer] 1930), 240.
Collective declaration drafted by RGL and signed by all members
of Le GJ. Repr. Ab39, Ab256, Ab275, Aa301, Ab317.

At38   Texts translated into Czech by Jindrich Horejsi, ibid.
Contains Ac10 and Ab11 (under title 'Le GJ. Úvodní manifest'),
Ab12.1 (under title 'Síla odříkání'), and Ac23.1 (under title 'Rozbití
dogmat. Manifest-polemika').

Ab39   Texts in *Le Grand Jeu*, 3 (automne [oct.] 1930).
Contains Ab37 (without title) and
.1 'La Prophétie des Rois Mages', 1-2. Repr. Ab256, Aa301,
Ab317.

.2 'L'Horrible Révélation...la seule', 3-17. Repr. Ab222,
Ab223, At245, Ab256, Aa296, Aa301, Ab317, At352.
.3 'Préambule', 19. Preface to Ab33.1. Repr. Ab256, Aa301,
Ab317, Ab339 (FMS).
.4 'Critique des critiques', 84-86. Repr. Ab256, Aa301, Ab317.
.5 'Laisser à d'autres...', 95. Repr. Ab256, Ab317.

Ac40   Collective declaration on Roger Vailland's withdrawal from Le GJ,
ibid., 2. Signed RD [*sic*], RGL [*sic*], and R[oger] V[ailland].
Repr. Ab256, Ab317, Ab366.

Ab41   'L'Enigme de la face', preface to *Exposition de figures humaines,
peintes par Joseph Sima*, catalogue of the exhibition 22 Nov. -13
Dec. 1930 at the Galerie Jacques Povolozki. Triple-folded pamphlet
with the text on the inner three faces (unpag.).
Repr. Ab45, Ab226, At245, Ab255, Ab275, Aa301.

1931

RENE DAUMAL

Ab42   'Poèmes', *NRF*, XXXVI, 210 (1 mars 1931), 351-54.
.1 'La Peau du monde', 351-52. Repr. Aa193, At239, Aa271,
At295.
.2 'Toujours en vain', 352-53. Repr. Aa193, At239, Aa271.
.3 'Vaine prière aux éléments', 353. Repr. Aa193, At239,
Aa271.
.4 'Le Partage', 353-54. Repr. Aa193, At239, Aa271.

Ab43   'L'Envers du décor', in a pamphlet of 16pp. (unpag.) entitled
'Hommage à Sima' accompanying *CdS*, VII, 131 (mai-juin 1931).
Repr. At93, Aa99, Aa193, Ab224, At239, Ab269, Aa271, Ab298.

Ab44   'Du fait ascétique comme réalité immédiate', *Anthologie des
philosophes contemporains* (ed. Arnaud Dandieu & Robert Aron,
Sagittaire, 8 oct. 1931, 542 pp.), 523-33.
Repr. Aa99, Aa193, Aa271, Aa288.

ROGER GILBERT-LECOMTE

Ab45   Ab41 in a pamphlet of 16pp. (unpag.) entitled 'Hommage à Sima'
accompanying *CdS*, VII, 131 (mai-juin 1931).

Ab46   'René Daumal', introduction to Ab44, 519-23. Repr. Aa301.

21

1932

RENE DAUMAL

Ac47   'Misère de la póesie. L'Affaire Aragon devant l'opinion publique', Editions surréalistes (mars 1932), 32pp. Tract by André Breton to which RD is a signatory.
Repr. Ac337.

Ab48   'Sur la musique hindoue', *NRF*, XXXVIII, 225 (1 juin 1932), 1088-99.
Repr. At52 (abr.), Aa265, Aa288, At355.

Ab49   'A propos d'Uday Shankar et de quelques autres Hindous', *CdS*, IX, 145 (nov. 1932), 709-18.
Repr. At54 (abr.), Aa184, Aa288, At355. See also Aa265.1 for draft version.

Ab50   Texts in *La Comédie psychologique. Précédé de A présent (Les tâches immédiates de la pensée révolutionnaire)*, by Carlo Suarès (Corti, 1932, 369pp.).
     .1 Letter to Suarès, Carlo, 6-7. Explains RD's reasons for not signing Ac51. Repr. Aa213 (369-70) where it is wrongly addressed to André Suarès, Ab267.
     .2 Annotations to *La Comédie psychologique, passim*. These are scattered throughout the text, and unsigned. Two extracts repr. Ab242.

Ac51   'A présent', ibid., 25-40. In collaboration with Carlo Suarès. The notes forming the basis of this text repr. Ac200, Ac204.

At52   'Music East and West', abridged version of Ab48 as part 1 of 'The Orient Unveiled. A Far Eastern Symposium' in *The Living Age* [Boston], 342 (1932), 526-32.

ROGER GILBERT-LECOMTE

Ac53   'Misère de la poesie. L'Affaire Aragon devant l'opinion publique', Editions surréalistes (mars 1932), 32pp. Tract by André Breton to which RGL is a signatory.
Repr. Ac340.

1933

RENE DAUMAL

At54 'Uday Shan-kar [*sic*] and the Hindu Dance', abridged version of Ab49 in *Hound and Horn* [Cambridge: Mass.], VI, 2 (Jan.-Mar. 1933), 288-92.
Translated by Vera Milanova.

Ab55 'A la Néante', *NRF*, XL, 233 (1 fév. 1933), 349. First 29 lines of a text fully published in Aa99.
Complete version repr. Aa193, Ab240, Aa271, Ab294, At295.

Ac56 'Protestez', tract by the 'Association des Ecrivains et Artistes Révolutionnaires' in *Feuille Rouge*, 2 (mars 1933), 2. RD is a signatory.
Repr. Ac337.

Ab57 Texts in 'L'Air du mois' in *NRF*, XLI, 242 (1 déc. 1933).
.1 'Valet d'argent', 937-38.
.2 'La Maternelle', 938.
.3 'Les Théâtres de marionnettes', 941.
.4 'Le Vivarium du Jardin des Plantes', 941.
.5 'Au Musée d'Ethnographie du Trocadéro [L'époque héroïque...]', 942-43.
.6 'Les Haricots modernes', 949.

Ab58 'Poème à Dieu et à l'homme', *Le Phare de Neuilly*, 1 [1933], 51-61.
Only a few copies were sold before the text was retracted by RD and a text by Petrus Borel inserted in its place. Extracts repr. Ab269. The full text repr. Aa261 (with documentation).

ROGER GILBERT-LECOMTE

Ab59 'L'Alchimie de l'œil; le cinéma, forme de l'esprit', *Cahiers Jaunes*, 4 ([1er trim.] 1933), 26-31.
Repr. Aa301.

Ac60 'Protestez', tract by the 'Association des Ecrivains et Artistes Révolutionnaires' in *Feuille Rouge*, 2 (mars 1933), 2. RGL is a signatory.
Repr. Ac340.

Aa61   *La Vie l'Amour la Mort le Vide et le Vent*. Editions des Cahiers libres, 25 oct. 1933, 128pp., 525 copies. With a 'prière d'insérer' by Léon Pierre-Quint (see Bb18).

The text has a preface and four sections:

.1 'Préface ou Le Drame de l'absence en un cœur éternel', 7-9. Repr. At245, Aa319.

[Section 1:] *La Vie*:

.2 'La Bonne Vie', 13-14. Repr. Aa205, At318, Aa319.

.3 'La Vie en rose', 15-16. Repr. Aa319.

.4 'Sombre histoire', 17-18. Repr. Aa319.

.5 'Le Drame dans une conscience enfantine', 19-20. Repr. Aa319.

.6 'Faux départ', 21. Repr. Aa319.

.7 'Le Chant malin du rat', 22-23. Repr. Aa319.

.8 'Poésie impure', 24. Repr. Aa319.

.9 'Monsieur Crabe, cet homme cadenas', 25-26. Repr. Aa319.

.10 'L'Histoire de France à l'école du soir', 27-32. Repr. Aa319.

.11 'Chanson française', 33-38. Repr. Aa205, Aa319.

.12 'La Vie masquée', 39-40. Repr. Aa205, At318, Aa319.

[Section 2:] *L'Amour*:

.13 'L'Epaisseur d'un poil', 43. Repr. Aa319.

.14 'Les Radis contiennent du radium', 44. Repr., Aa319.

.15 'La Sagesse inutile', 45. Repr. Aa319.

.16 'Les Frontières de l'amour', 46. Repr. Aa319.

.17 'L'Art de la danse', 47-52. Repr. Aa319.

.18 'Faire l'amour', 53-57. Repr. Aa319.

.19 'Sacre et massacre de l'amour', 59-69. Repr. Aa205, Aa220, At245, Aa319.

[Section 3:] *La Mort*:

.20 'Un soir', 73. Repr. Aa319.

.21 'La Nénie du bon vieux', 74-75. Repr. Aa319.

.22 'Formule palingénésique', 76. Repr. At245, Aa319.

.23 'Absence vorace', 77-78. Repr. At245, Aa319. Another version Ab263.7.

.24 'La Mort nocturne', 79. Repr. Aa319.

.25 'Le Noyé noyau', 80-81. Repr. Aa280.80, Aa319.

.26 'Le Pendu', 82. Repr. Aa319.

.27 'Suppositions mortelles', 83-84. Repr. Aa319.

.28 'La Tête à l'envers', 85-86. Repr. At245, Aa319.

.29 'L'Aile d'endormir', 87-88. Repr. At245, Aa319.

.30 'Le Fils de l'os', 89-94. Repr. At245, Aa319.

.31 'Le Fils de l'os parle', 95-96. Repr. At245, Aa319.

.32 'Le Grand et le Petit Guignol', 97-98. Repr. Aa205, At318, Aa319.

[Section 4:] *Le Vide et le Vent*:
.33 'Le Vide de verre', 101-02. Repr. Ab145, Aa319.
.34 'Je n'ai pas peur du vent', 103-09. Repr. At245, Aa319.
.35 'Le Feu du vent', 110. Repr. Aa319.
.36 'Quand viendra le jour du grand vent', 111-13. Repr. Aa319.
.37 'Le Vent d'après le vent d'avant', 114-16. Repr. At245, Aa319.
.38 'L'Incantation perpétuelle', 117. Repr. At245, Aa319.

1934

RENE DAUMAL

Ab62   'French Letter', *Hound and Horn* [Cambridge: Mass.], VII, 2 (Jan.-Mar. 1934), 267-70. In English; with indication 'Paris, Late Summer, 1933'.

Ab63   Texts in 'L'Air du mois' in *NRF*, XLII, 244 (1 jan. 1934).
.1 'Au Musée des Colonies', 153.
.2 'Livres d'enfants', 154-55.
.3 'Une invention pataphysique', 156.

Ab64   'Les Ballets Joos', in 'L'Air du mois' in *NRF*, XLII, 245 (1 fév. 1934), 398-99.

Ab65   Texts in 'L'Air du mois' in *NRF*, XLII, 246 (1 mars 1934).
.1 'L'Education de l'homme', 578-79.
.2 'Au Musée d'Ethnographie du Trocadéro [On ne peut quand même pas...]', 579-80.

Ab66   'Jaques-Dalcroze [*sic*], éducateur', in 'Notes' in *NRF*, XLII, 247 (1 avr. 1934), 723-27.
Repr. Aa184, Ab192 (abr.), Aa288.

Ab67   Texts in *NRF*, XLII, 248 (1 mai 1934).
.1 'Le Non-dualisme de Spinoza ou la dynamite philosophique', 769-87. Repr. Aa184, At251, Aa288.
In section 'L'Air du mois':
.2 'Uday Sankar [*sic*]', 897-98.
.3 'Un film assassiné', 898-99. Repr. Aa184.

Ab68   '*Le Livre des morts tibétain*', *CdS*, XI, 162 (juin 1934), 371-77.
Repr. Aa184, Aa287, At355.

25

Ab69   Texts in *NRF*, XLII, 249 (1 juin 1934).
        In section 'Revue des livres':
        .1 '*Œuvres complètes de Rabelais* publiées par Jacques
           Boulenger', 1031.
        .2 '*Les Remarques sur la langue françoise* de Vaugelas,
           publiées par Jeanne Streicher', 1031-32.
        In section 'L'Air du mois':
        .3 'Livres d'images de Max Ernst', 1048.
        .4 'Quelques hindous', 1050-51.
        .5 'La Pataphysique du mois [Sir Arthur Eddington...]',
           1051-52.

Ab70   Texts in 'L'Air du mois' in *NRF*, XLIII, 250 (1 juill. 1934).
        .1 'La Grande Expérience', 151.
        .2 'Honte (contre-plan) (Salle Pleyel)', 151-52.
        .3 'Helba Huara', 155-56.
        .4 'La Pataphysique du mois [Les peupliers ont jeté...]',
           158-59.

Ab71   Texts in 'L'Air du mois' in *NRF*, XLIII, 251 (1 août 1934).
        .1 'Un nouvel art de l'écran', 317-18.
        .2 'La Pataphysique du mois [Il y a encore 2 cases...]', 318.
        .3 'La Psychose du passeport', 319.

Ab72   Texts in *NRF*, XLIII, 252 (1 sept. 1934).
        In section 'Revue des livres':
        .1 '*Les Religions révélées*, par Henri Roger', 465-66.
        In section 'L'Air du mois':
        .2 'Danse sacrée', 474.

Ab73   Texts in 'L'Air du mois' in *NRF*, XLIII, 253 (1 oct. 1934).
        .1 'L'Eden économique', 633.
        .2 'Genève en septembre', 635-36.

Ab74   'Le Mouvement dans l'éducation intégrale de l'homme' [part 1],
        Régénération, 54 (oct. 1934), 28-30.
        Repr. Ab242, Aa288.

Ab75   'La Pataphysique du mois [L'astronomie nous apporte...]', in
        'L'Air du mois' in *NRF*, XLIII, 254 (1 nov. 1934), 798-99.

Ab76   'Le Mouvement dans l'éducation intégrale de l'homme' [part 2],
        Régénération, 55 (nov. 1934), 14-17.
        Repr. Ab242, Aa288.

Ab77   'La Pataphysique du mois [Attention, les sens!...]', in 'L'Air du mois' in *NRF*, XLIII, 255 (1 déc. 1934), 949-50.

Ab78   'Têtes fatiguées', *Présence* [Genève], 4 (1934-35), 20-26. Repr. Aa287.

ROGER GILBERT-LECOMTE

Ac79   'Appel à la lutte', Surrealist tract dated 10 fév. 1934 to which RGL is a signatory.
Repr. Ac80, Ac170, Ac340.

Ac80   Ac79 in 'Intervention surréaliste', *Documents* [Bruxelles], 34 (1934), 5-6.

1935

RENE DAUMAL

Ab81   'La Pataphysique du mois [Sentiment général catastrophique...]', in 'L'Air du mois' in *NRF*, XLIV, 257 (1 fév. 1935), 332.

Ab82   '*Vers l'abandon des philosophies discursives*, par Julien Favre', in 'Notes bibliographiques' in *Présence* [Genève], III, 2 (mars 1935), 37-38.

Ab83   'Les Limites du langage philosophique et les savoirs traditionnels', *Recherches Philosophiques*, 4 (1934-35 [avr. 1935]), 209-231.
Repr. Aa184, At251, Aa287.

Ab84   Texts in 'Notes' in *NRF*, XLIV, 260 (1 mai 1935).
.1 '*Pour la poésie*, par Jean Cassou', 764-65.
Repr. Ab277.
.2 '*La Mythologie primitive* par L. Lévy-Bruhl', 773-77.
Repr. Aa287.

As85   'La Nature essentielle de la poésie [*Sâhitya-Darpana*, ch.1]', *Présence* [Genève], III, 4 (mai 1935), 11-17.
Repr. At251, Aa265.

Ab86   'Comme dit la chanson', *La Bête Noire*, 3 (1 juin 1935), 3.
Incorporated in Aa116. Repr. Aa193.

Ab87   'A propos de nouvelles religions et au revoir!', *La Bête Noire*, 4 (1 juill. 1935), 6.
Repr. Ab232, Ab277.

Ab88   '*Les Cenci* d'Antonin Artaud et *Autour d'une mère* de J.-L. Barrault', in 'Coups de Théâtre' in *Ecrits du Nord* [Bruxelles], I, 2 (juill. 1935), 477-82. Repr. Ab338.

Ab89   'Les Broderies de Marie Monnier', in 'L'Air du mois' in *NRF*, XLV, 262 (1 juill. 1935), 154-56.

Ab90   'La Vie des Basiles', *Mesures*, 3 (15 juill. 1935), 39-56.
Repr. Aa184, At251, Aa287.

Ab91   Texts in 'Notes' in *NRF*, XLV, 264 (1 sept. 1935).
.1 '*Linguistique générale et linguistique française*, par Ch. Bailly', 434-36. Repr. Aa184, Aa287.
.2 '*L'Evolution du sens des mots depuis le XVIe siècle*, par Edmond Huguet', 458-59.

As92   'L'Origine du Théâtre de Bharata (commenté et traduit par RD) [*Nâtya-çâstra*]', *Mesures*, 4 (15 oct. 1935), 133-160.
Repr. As212, At251, Aa265, At355.

1936

RENE DAUMAL

At93   Ab43 translated into Czech under title 'Opak dekoru', in *Zivot* [Praha], 14 (unor [Feb.] 1936), 67.

Ab94   '*Fables de mon jardin* par Georges Duhamel', in 'Notes' in *NRF*, XLVI, 272 (1 mai 1936), 799-801.

Ab95   'Gaspilleurs de ciel', in 'L'Air du mois' in *NRF*, XLVI, 273 (1 juin 1936), 998-99.

Ab96   Texts in *NRF*, XLVII, 275 (1 août 1936).
In section 'Notes':
.1 '*Le Bouddhisme, ses doctrines et ses méthodes*, par Alexandra David-Neel', 387-89. Repr. Aa287, At355.
In section 'L'Air du mois':
.2 'Notre révolution', 407-08.
.3 'Entre deux chaises', 413-15. Repr. Ab277, Aa287, At325.

Ab97   'Sur le scientisme et la révolution', *Europe*, 164 (15 août 1936), 556-61.
Repr. Aa184, Aa261 (abr.), Aa287.

Ab98   '*Histoire de la civilisation africaine*, par Léo Frobenius', in 'Notes' in *NRF*, XLVII, 276 (1 sept. 1936), 553-55.
Repr. Aa184, Aa287.

Aa99   *Le Contre Ciel. Lithographie originale d'Etienne Cournault.* Editions de l'Université de Paris, 22 sept. 1936, 102pp., 315 copies. With the indication on 8 'JULIEN BENDA ANDRE GIDE JEAN GIRAUDOUX ADRIENNE MONNIER JEAN PAULHAN ANDRE SUARES PAUL VALERY MEMBRES DU COMITE LITTERAIRE DE LA SOCIETE DES AMIS DE LA BIBLIO-THEQUE LITTERAIRE ANTOINE JACQUES DOUCET ONT DECERNE LE PRIX DOUCET A RENE DAUMAL POUR LE CONTRE CIEL LE NEUF JUILLET 1935' [*sic*] and on 101 'ce livre édité par la société des amis de la Bibliothèque littéraire Antoine Jacques Doucet.' Collection repr. Aa193, Aa271. Has three sections preceded by an *Avertissement* (9):
[Section 1:]
   .1 'Clavicules d'un grand jeu poétique', 13-55. Nos. 1-12 previously published as Ab44. Whole section repr. Aa193, At220a, Aa271, Aa288.
[Section 2:] *La Mort et son homme* contains Ab29.7, Ab29.8, the complete version of Ab55 and
   .2 'La Peau du fantôme', 59-60. Repr. Aa193, Aa271.
   .3 'Le Grand Jour des Morts', 60-63. Repr. Aa193, Aa271.
   .4 'Nénie', 67-70. Repr. Aa193, Aa271.
   .5 'Perséphone, c'est-à-dire double-issue', 70-72. Draft version of this text published in Ab185. Repr. Aa193, At239, Aa271.
   .6 'Nymphe liminaire', 72-73. Repr. Aa193, Aa271.
   .7 'La Fameuse Surprise', 73-75. Repr. Aa193, Aa271.
   .8 'La Désillusion', 75-76. Repr. Aa193, Aa271.
   .9 'Après', 76-77. Repr. Aa193, Aa271, At295.
   .10 'Lc Scrment de fidélité', 77-80. Repr. Aa193, Aa271.
   .11 'Triste petit train de vie', 84-85. Repr. Aa193, Aa271.
   .12 'Froidement', 85-86. Repr. Aa193, Aa271.
[Section 3:] *Le ciel est convexe* contains Ab14.6, Ab29.2, Ab43 and
   .13 'Brève révélation sur la mort et le chaos', 93-94. Repr. Aa193, Aa271.
   .14 'Comment tout recommence', 96-97. Repr. Aa193, Aa271.

Ab100   '*Le Secret de la Grande Pyramide*, par C. Barbarin', in 'Notes' in *NRF*, XLVII, 279 (1 déc. 1936), 1078-80. Repr. Aa184.

1937

RENE DAUMAL

Ab101   '*Hermès* (Numéro consacré à Maître Eckehart, juillet)', in 'Notes' in *NRF,* XLIX, 289 (1 oct. 1937), 685-86. Repr. Aa184.

Ab102   Texts in 'Notes' in *NRF*, XLIX, 291 (1 déc. 1937).
.1 'Scènes de *Faust*, par le Gœtheanum', 1029.
.2 'Habimah, le théâtre hébreu de Palestine', 1029-31. Repr. Aa184.

Ae103   *Meurtre en noir [Murder in black], F.D. Grierson. Roman policier. Traduit de l'anglais par Simon Martin-Chauffier et RD.* Librairie des Champs-Elysées, coll. 'Le Masque', no.223, 1937, 256pp.

ROGER GILBERT-LECOMTE

Aa104   *Le Miroir noir.* Editions Sagesse, coll. 'Les Feuilles de Sagesse', no.57, [1937]. Pamphlet of 8pp. (unpag.); no. of copies unknown (only indication is 'il a été tiré à part six exemplaires').
.1 'Chant de mort Cristal d'ouragan', [3]. Repr. Aa319.
.2 'Dans les yeux de la nuit', [3-4]. Repr. Aa319.
.3 'La Sainte Enfance ou Suppression de la naissance', [4-5]. Repr. Ab172, Aa205, Aa319, At372.
.4 'Deuil d'azur', [6]. Repr. Aa205, At318, Aa319.
.5 'La Chanson du prisonnier', [6-7]. Repr. Aa205, Aa319.
.6 'Je veux être confondu...ou La Halte du prophète', [7-8]. Repr. Ab145, Ab160, Aa205, Aa319.
.7 'Testament', [8]. Repr. Aa205, Aa319.

1938

RENE DAUMAL

Ab105   '*Encyclopédie française (V). Les êtres vivants*', in 'Notes' in *NRF*, L, 293 (1 fév. 1938), 319-21. Repr. Aa287.

Ab106   'Sur le tantrisme hindou', in 'Notes' in *NRF*, L, 294 (1 mars 1938), 510-11. Repr. Ab277.

Ab107   'Les Pouvoirs de la parole dans la poétique hindoue', *Mesures*, 2
         (15 avr. 1938), 79-106.
         Repr. At251, Aa265, Aa287.

Ae108   *Mort dans l'après-midi [Death in the afternoon], Ernest*
         Hemingway. Traduit de l'anglais par RD. Gallimard, nrf, 15 avr.
         1938, 306pp.
         Repr. Ae173, Ae179, Ae216, Ae228, Ae231, Ae236, Ae289.

Ab109   'Les Souvenirs de l'Inde du Chevalier Gentil', *Verve*, 3
         (1 juin 1938), 40 & 44.
         Draft version published as Ab345.8.

Ab110   'La Pataphysique du mois [A Saint-Brieuc...]', in 'L'Air du mois',
         in *NRF*, LI, 298 (1 juill. 1938), 167-70.
         Repr. Aa287.

Ab111   Texts in 'Notes bibliographiques' in *Hermès* [Bruxelles],
         2 (oct. 1938).
           .1 'André Rolland de Renéville, *L'Expérience poétique*', 158-61.
           Repr. Aa184, Aa287.
           .2 'Jacques Bacot, *La Vie de Marpa, le "Traducteur"*', 162-63.
           Repr. Aa184, Aa287, At355.

Ab112   '*Deux textes tibétains sur la conversion des oiseaux*', in 'Notes' in
         NRF, LI, 301 (1 oct. 1938), 681-84.
         Repr. Aa184, Aa287, At355.

Ab113   'Les Dernières Paroles du poète', *Europe*, 192 (15 déc. 1938),
         456-60.
         Repr. Aa193, Ab240, Aa271, Ab294.

ROGER GILBERT-LECOMTE

Ab114   'Max Hunziker', in 'L'Air du mois' in *NRF*, LI, 299 (1 août
         1938), 342-43.
         Repr. Aa356.

1939

RENE DAUMAL

Ab115   'La Pataphysique du mois [Les révélations du Docteur

Faustroll...]', in 'L'Air du mois' in *NRF*, LII, 304 (1 jan. 1939), 182-84.
Repr. Aa287.

Aa116   *La Grande Beuverie*. Gallimard, nrf, coll. 'Métamorphoses', no.66, 28 jan. 1939 [copyright 1938], 160pp.
Contains Ab86. Repr. Aa155, Aa194, Aa244, Aa260, At272, Aa310, At332, At333, Aa336, At349, Aa364. Short extracts repr. Aa193, Ab240, Ab294.

Ae117   *Moi et Moi [My Selves], N. Lucas & E. Graham. Roman traduit de l'anglais par RD*. Gallimard, 21 mars 1939, 286pp.

Ab118   '*Le Yoga tibétain et les doctrines secrètes ou Les Sept Livres de la Sagesse du Grand Sentier*, suivant la traduction du Lâma Kasi Dawa Samdup', in 'Notes bibliographiques' in *Hermès* [Bruxelles], 3 (avr. 1939), 158-60.
Repr. Aa184, Aa287.

Ab119   Texts in *Verve*, no. sp. 'La Figure humaine', 5-6 (juill.-août 1939).
    .1 'L'Envers de la tête', 109-10. Repr. Aa184, At251, Aa287.
    Extract repr. Ab240, Ab294.
    .2 'Jésus devant Pilate (Matthieu 27)', 164. Uncredited commentary on a plate by Jean Foucquet from Etienne Chevalier's *Livre d'heures*. Repr. Aa193, Ab240, Aa287, Ab294.

Ab120   'La Pataphysique du mois [Etes-vous panspermiste?..]', in 'L'Air du mois' in *NRF*, LIII, 311 (1 août 1939), 345-46.
Repr. Aa287.

Ab121   '*Hymnes et prières du Véda*, traduits par Louis Renou', in 'Notes' in *NRF*, LIII, 312 (1 sept. 1939), 504-06.
Repr. Aa287, At355.

Ab122   '*Anthologie juive*, par Edmond Fleg', in 'Notes' in *NRF*, LIII, 313 (1 oct. 1939), 653-54.
Repr. Aa184, Aa287.

ROGER GILBERT-LECOMTE

Ab123   'La Lézarde', *Mercure de France*, CCXC, 977 (1 mars 1939), 475-82.
Extract repr. Ab168. Whole version repr. Aa205, Aa301.

1940

RENE DAUMAL

Ab124 'La Pataphysique du mois [Avec des ruses de fourmilière...]', in
       'L'Air du mois' in *NRF*, LIV, 316 (1 jan. 1940), 139-41.
       Repr. Aa287.

Ab125 'Le Mont Analogue [ch.1]', *Mesures*, 1 (15 jan. 1940), 39-54.
       Ch.1 of Aa180. With an introduction and conclusion by RD
       (39 & 54); this version repr. At284, Aa344.

Ab126 'La Guerre sainte', *Fontaine* [Alger], 11 (oct.-nov. 1940), 108-13.
       Repr. Aa127, Ab164, Aa193, Ab235, Ab240, Aa271, At284,
       Ab294.

Aa127 *La Guerre sainte*. Ab126 in 'tirage à part', Fontaine [Alger], coll.
       'Analecta', no.4 (10 déc. 1940), 8pp.

1941

RENE DAUMAL

As128 'La Connaissance de Soi [*sic*]. Extrait de la *Brihadâranyaka
       Upanishad*, IV, 4, 10-21', *CdS*, no. sp. 'Message actuel de l'Inde',
       236 (juin-juill. 1941), 37-38.
       Repr. Aa265, Aa271, At284, At355.

Ab129 'Pour approcher l'art poétique hindou', ibid., 253-67.
       Repr. Ac176, Aa184, At251, Aa265, At284, Aa287, At355.

Ab130 'Quelques poètes français du XXVe [*sic*] siècle', *Fontaine* [Alger],
       14 (juin 1941), 338-44.
       Repr. Aa184, At284, Aa287.

Ab131 'L'Histoire des hommes-creux et de la Rose-amère', *CdS*, 239 (oct.
       1941), 450-53.
       Later incorporated in Aa180. Repr. Ab240, Ab294.

Ab132 'Le Message de la *Bhagavad-Gîtâ*, par Jean Herbert', *CdS*, 241
       (déc. 1941), 669-71.
       Repr. Aa184, Aa287.

Ab133 'La Pataphysique des fantômes', *Fontaine* [Alger], III, 16 (déc. 1941), 124-29.
Another version in Aa184. Both versions repr. Aa287.

ROGER GILBERT-LECOMTE

Ab134 '*L'Arbre de visages*, par Marcel Jouhandeau', in 'Notes' in *NRF*, LV, 333 (1 nov. 1941), 624-26.
Extract repr. Aa205.26, Aa301.38; complete version repr. Aa356.

1942

RENE DAUMAL

Ab135 'Poésie noire, poésie blanche', *Fontaine* [Alger], no. sp. 'De la poésie comme exercice spirituel', 19-20 (mars-avr. 1942), 168-72.
Repr. Aa184, At251, Aa271, At284, Aa287.

As136 Various texts, ibid., 207-18 under title 'Quelques textes sanskrits sur la poésie'. With the indication 'Textes traduits et commentés par RD'. Followed by a 'Notice sur les auteurs et ouvrages cités'.
Repr. Aa271, At284, At355.
  .1 '*Sâhitya-darpana*, 1ère section, début', 207-09.
  .2 '*Nâtya-çâstra*, 1ère lecture', 209-11.
  .3 '*Sâhitya-darpana*, 1ère section, suite', 211-14.
  .4 '*Nâtya-çâstra*, 6ème lecture, 32-33', 214-15.
  .5 '*Rasataranginî*, 6', 215-16.
  .6 'Bhartrihari [III,15]', 216. Repr. Ab345.
  .7 '*Sâhitya-darpana*, 3ème section, 33 sqq.', 216-17.

Ab137 'Le Philosophe', *Pyrénées* [Toulouse], no. sp. 'Lanza del Vasto', 5 (mars-avr. 1942), 517-33.
Repr. Ab197.

Ae138 Extracts from *Essays on Zen Buddhism* by Daisetz Teitaro Suzuki under title 'Un maître de liberté' in *Fontaine* [Alger], IV, 21 (mai 1942), 28-36. With an introduction by RD (28-29).
Repr. Ab345. Contains translations in the following order of:
  .1 'The koan exercise (Second series, essay 1; part I, 4, iv, 6)', incorporated in Ae154.
  .2 'The secret message of Bodhidharma (Second series, Essay 2; 12)', incorporated in Ae165.
  .3 'The meditation hall and the ideals of the monkish discipline (First series, Essay 7; 10)', incorporated in Ae153.

Ab139   '*L'Apprentissage de la ville*, par Luc Dietrich', in 'Chroniques', ibid., 107-10.
Repr. Ab235(abr.), Ab277, Aa287.

Ab140   'Symbole et allégorie', *Fusées* [Marseille], 2 (7 juin 1942), 113-16. Answer to Bb29. Repr. Ab277, Ab345.

Ab141   'Mémorables', *Fontaine* [Alger], IV, 23 ([juill.] 1942), 233-34. Repr. Aa193, Ab235, Ab240, At251, Aa271, Ab294, At299.

Ab142   'Lettre sur l'art de mentir', *Fusées* [Marseille], no. sp. 'Sincérité', 4-5 (août-sept. 1942), 16-18.
Repr. Ab277, Ab345.

Ae143   'L'Exercice du koan', *CdS*, XIX, 250 (nov. 1942), 39-54. Extract from *Essays on Zen Buddhism* by Daisetz Teitaro Suzuki (Second series, 'The koan exercise', part I, 8-9). With an introduction by RD (39-40). Incorporated without the introduction, and with minor changes in Ae154. This version repr. Ab345.

Ac144   *L'Enseignement de Râmakrishna. Recueil des paroles de Shrî Râmakrishna Paramahamsa. Groupées et annotées par Jean Herbert avec la collaboration de Marie Honegger-Durand et P. Seshadri Iyer* [Second edition]. Adrien-Maisonneuve [Paris] & Delachaux et Niestlé [Neuchâtel: Suisse], 1942, iv & 650 & xxii pp. The preface by J. Herbert indicates (12) that RD collaborated for the Glossary (671-83), not contained in the first edition. Repr. Ac175.

ROGER GILBERT-LECOMTE

Ab145   'Poèmes' , in *NRF*, 341 (1 juill. 1942), 63-64. Contains Aa61.33 (under title 'Palais du vide') and Aa104.6.

Ac146   'Le Romantisme allemand', *Comoedia*, 54 (4 juill. 1942), 7. In collaboration with Arthur Adamov. Repr. Aa356.

Ac147   'Les Pressentiments d'une métamorphose de l'esprit humain', *Comoedia*, 55 (11 juill. 1942), 7. In collaboration with Arthur Adamov. Repr. Aa356.

Ac148   'Novalis ou le message du poète: rendre à l'homme sa noblesse primitive', *Comoedia*, 60 (15 août 1942), 5. In collaboration with Arthur Adamov. Repr. Aa356.

Ac149   'Mörike ou la voix de l'amour', *Comoedia*, 73 (14 nov. 1942), 7.
In collaboration with Arthur Adamov. Repr. Aa356.

1943

RENE DAUMAL

Ac150   'Dialogue du style', *CdS*, XIX, 252 (jan. 1943), 11-16.
In collaboration with Lanza del Vasto. Repr. Aa287.

Ab151   'Note', *Fontaine* [Alger], V, 29 ([août]) 1943), 380-81.

Ab152   'Le Mot et la mouche', *CdS*, XIX, 262 (déc. 1943), 1015-17.
Introduced by a letter to Léon-Gabriel Gros. Repr. At251, Aa287,
Ab348.

Ae153   *Essais sur le Bouddhisme Zen [Essays on Zen Buddhism].
Deuxième volume, Daisetz Teitaro Suzuki. Traduction de Pierre
Sauvageot et RD.* Adrien-Maisonneuve [Paris] & Delachaux et
Niestlé [Neuchâtel: Suisse], coll. 'Bouddhisme et Jaïnisme',
1943, 227 & xx pp.
Contains Ae138.3. Repr. Ae157, Ae190, Ae285.

Ae154   *Essais sur le Bouddhisme Zen [Essays on Zen Buddhism].
Troisième volume, Daisetz Teitaro Suzuki. Traduction de RD.*
Adrien-Maisonneuve [Paris] & Delachaux et Niestlé [Neuchâtel:
Suisse], coll. 'Bouddhisme et Jaïnisme', 1943, iv & 288pp.
Contains Ae138.1, Ae143. Repr. Ae158, Ae206, Ae286.

Aa155   Second edition of Aa116. Gallimard, coll. 'Metamorphoses',
no.8, 20 déc. 1943, 160pp., 1650 copies (550 of which are in
hardback, 'reliés d'après la maquette de Paul Bonet', no
collection specified).

1944

RENE DAUMAL

Ae156   *La Kena Upanishad, Shrî Aurobindo. Traduction française de
Camille Rao, RD, et Jean Herbert.* Adrien-Maisonneuve [Paris] &
Delachaux et Niestlé [Neuchâtel: Suisse], coll. 'Grands maîtres

spirituels dans l'Inde contemporaine', mars 1944, 104 pp. Repr. Ae174, Ae199, Ae279.

Ae157   Ae153, *Deuxième édition revue et corrigée*, 1944.

Ae158   Ae154, second edition, 1944.

ROGER GILBERT-LECOMTE

Ab159   'Poèmes de RGL', in *CdS*, XXI, 266 (juin-juill. 1944), 402-04.
With texts by Pierre Minet and Léon Pierre-Quint (see Bb30).
Contains Aa104.6 and
　　.1 'L'Eternité en un clin d'œil', 402. Repr. Ab171, Aa205,
　　　　Aa319, Ab321.
　　.2 'La Tête couronnée', 403. Repr. Ab162, Ab171, Aa205,
　　　　Aa319, Ab328, At372.

Ab160   Aa104.6 in André Rolland de Renéville, *L'Univers de la Parole*
(Gallimard, nrf, 15 nov. 1944, 212pp.), 163-64.

1945

RENE DAUMAL

Ab161   'Quelques réponses de RD à Luc Dietrich', *CdS*, XXIII, 272
([août] 1945), 512-17.
With an introduction by V[éra] D[aumal]. Repr. Aa184.

ROGER GILBERT-LECOMTE

Ab162   Texts in *L'Heure Nouvelle*, [1] (1945).
Contains Ab159.2 and
　　.1 'Les Quatre Eléments', 15. Repr. Ab171, Aa205, Aa319,
　　　　Aa356.
　　.2 'Acte de dépossession (tension)', 34. Repr. Ab171, Aa205,
　　　　Aa301 [232].
　　.3 'Raison-Choc-Système', 35. Repr. Ab171, Aa205,
　　　　Aa301 [233].
Under overall title 'La Révélation de la Troisième Heure', the
following, introduced by Arthur Adamov (see Bb34).
　　.4 'Histoire de l'esprit humain', 36. Repr. Aa301 [229].
　　.5 'La Troisième naissance de l'homme', 36. Repr. Aa205,
　　　　Aa301 [230].

.6 'Le Mystère de la trinité', 36-37. Repr. Aa205 (abr.),
Aa301 [229-30].

.7 'Le Fondement de la troisième morale', 37. Repr. Aa205,
Aa301 [230-31].

1946

RENE DAUMAL

Ab163   'Une expérience fondamentale', *Les Cahiers de la Pléiade*,
[1] (avr. 1946), 166-73.
Repr. Aa184, At251, Ab269, Aa287, At371. Extracts repr. Ab240,
Ab242, Ab294.

Ab164   'Deux textes de RD', in *Fontaine* [Alger], IX, 52 (mai 1946),
788-807.
Commemoration presented by M[ax]-P[ol] F[ouchet], accompanied
by an article by Henri Hell and a bio-bibliography (see Bb37).
Contains Ab126 and
.1 'Le Mont-Analogue [ch.4]', 794-807. Ch.4 of Aa180.

Ae165   *Essais sur le Bouddhisme Zen [Essays on Zen Buddhism].*
Quatrième volume, Daisetz Teitaro Suzuki. Traduction de RD.
Adrien-Maisonneuve [Paris] & Delachaux et Niestlé
[Neuchâtel: Suisse], coll. 'Bouddhisme et Jaïnisme', 1946, iv
& 181 & 7pp.
Contains Ae138.2. Repr. Ae206.

ROGER GILBERT-LECOMTE

Ab166   Texts under title 'Notes', in *Arts et Lettres*, 1 (mars 1946), 23-26.
With an introduction by Arthur Adamov (see Bb35).
.1 'Notes de bord', 24-25. Repr. Ab171, Aa205, Aa301
[173-74].
.2 'Notes pour l'univers des mythes', 25-26. Repr. Ab171,
Aa205, Aa296, Aa301 [176-77].

Ab167   Ab12.1 in *Troisième Convoi*, 3 (nov. 1946), 27-33.

Ab168   Texts in *L'Heure Nouvelle*, 2 (1946), 31-33 & 70-72.
Contains extracts from Ab123 (31-33) and the following under the
title 'Notes':
.1 'Ce n'est rien...', 70. Repr. Aa205, Aa301 [174-75].
.2 'Vision par l'épiphyse. Nous vivons...', 70-71. Repr. Aa205,
Aa296, Aa301 [169].

.3 'L'arbre dans l'homme...', 71. Repr. Aa205, Aa296, Aa301 [121].

.4 'La cage du thorax...', 71. Repr. Aa205, Aa296, Aa301 [171].

.5 'Echos, rumeurs', 71-72. Repr. Aa205, Aa296, Aa301 [171-72].

1947

RENE DAUMAL

Ab169 'La Mère Mot [later title "Le Père Mot"]', *La Licorne*, 1 (print. [mars] 1947), 151-52. Repr. Aa193, At251, Aa271, Aa287.

1948

ROGER GILBERT-LECOMTE

Ac170 Ac79 in Maurice Nadeau, *Histoire du surréalisme, II. Documents surréalistes* (Seuil, collection 'Pierre vives', 2e trim. 1948, 400pp.), 251-53.

Ab171 Texts under title 'D'un cahier posthume' in *Mercure de France*, CCCIV, 1022 (1 oct. 1948), 261-68.
With an introduction by Marthe Robert and Arthur Adamov (see Bb46). Contains Ab159.1, Ab159.2, Ab162.1, Ab162.2, Ab162.3 (under title 'Raison-Système-Choc du chaos'), Ab166.1, Ab166.2, Ab168.1 (under title 'Au fond de tout'), and
.1 'Vertige', 261. Repr. Aa319, At372. FMS in Ab328.
.2 'Retour de flamme', 263-64. Repr. Aa205, Aa301, At318.
Nine brief notes under collective title 'Phrases':
.3 'L'homme éternel...', 264. Repr. Aa205, Aa301 [172].
.4 'Regarder à se crever les yeux...', 264. Repr. Aa205, Aa301 [175].
.5 'La mince pellicule...', 264. Repr. Aa205, Aa301 [173].
.6 'Je brûle...', 264. Repr. Aa205, Aa301 [173].
.7 'Il n'y avait plus entre moi...', 264. Repr. Aa205, Aa301 [172].
.8 'Je sentais pourtant...', 264. Repr. Aa205, Aa301 [205].
.9 'Le drame auquel j'assiste...', 264. Repr. Aa301 [205].
.10 'Le bruit des oiseaux...', 265. Repr. Aa301 [205].
.11 'La vie, un mélange...', 265. Repr. Aa301 [198].

Ab172 Aa104.3 in *84*, 3-4 (1948), 76-77.

1949

RENE DAUMAL

Ae173   New edition of Ae108 'traduit de l'américain par RD', Gallimard, 29 avr. 1949, 304pp., 1040 copies.

Ae174   Ae156 in *Shri Aurobindo, Œuvres complètes (2). Trois Upanishads (Isha, Kena, Mundaka).* Albin Michel, coll. 'Spiritualités vivantes', 'série Hindouisme', mai 1949, 288pp. (117-235).

Ac175   New edition of Ac144. Albin Michel, coll. 'Spiritualités vivantes', 'série Hindouisme', sept. 1949, xv & 720pp. (Glossary on 691-703; RD uncredited in preface).

Ac176   Two texts in *CdS*, no.sp. 'Approches de l'Inde' (30 nov. 1949; ed. Jacques Masui).
Contains Ab129 and
    .1 'Tableau du développement de la tradition hindoue', 25-35. In collaboration with Jacques Masui.

ROGER GILBERT-LECOMTE

Ab177   'Rêve de mort [Eveillé en sursaut...]', *84*, 10-11 (1949), 402-03. Repr. Ab196, Aa205, Aa319 [197-98].

1951

RENE DAUMAL

Ab178   Abridged version of Ab14.7 under title 'René Guénon', in *CdS*, 12 (print.-été [10 juill. 1951]), 36-37.

Ae179   Second edition of Ae173, 2 oct. 1951, 304pp.

1952

RENE DAUMAL

Aa180   *Le Mont Analogue. Préface de [André] Rolland de Renéville. Récit véridique.* Gallimard, nrf, 24 mars 1952, 216pp.

With a postface by Véra Daumal (see Bb47 for this and the preface). Repr. At218, At219, At220b, Aa221, At229, At249, At250, Aa252, Aa290, At300, Aa344, At353, At354, At361a, At369. Short extracts repr. Aa193, Ab240, Ab294. Contains Ab131 and

.1 Letter to Christoflour, Raymond dated 24 fév. 1940, 20-22. Repr. Aa221, At229, Aa252, At284, Aa290.

.2 Extract from diary, *circa* 1939, 20-22. Repr. Aa221, At229 Aa252, Aa290, Aa344.

.3 Extract from notes on *Le Mont Analogue*, 193-96. Repr. At218, At219, Aa221, At229, At249, At250, Aa252, Aa290 At300.

.4 Letter to Daumal, Véra, undated (extract), 197. Repr. Aa193, At218, At219, Aa221, At229, Ab240, At249, Aa252, Aa290, Ab294, At300.

.5 'Notes retrouvées dans les papiers de RD', 199-210. Repr. At218, At219, Aa221, At229, At249, At250, Aa252, Aa290, At300, Aa344.

Ab181   'Lettre inédite à Jean Paulhan' (undated), *Synthèses,* [Bruxelles], 79 (déc. 1952), 206-10. Repr. Aa287.

1953

RENE DAUMAL

Ab182   Texts in *France-Asie* [Saigon], no.sp. 'René Guénon', VIII, 80 (jan. 1953).
Contains Ab14.7 under title 'Sur les livres de René Guénon' and
.1 'Lettre inédite de RD adressée le 16 sept. 1942 à Mme Geneviève Lief', 1256.

Ab183   'Sous un jour plus intime', *NRF*, I, 5 (1 mai 1953), 938-42. Repr. Aa184, Ab202, Aa213, Aa288.

Aa184   *Chaque fois que l'aube paraît. Essais et notes I.* Gallimard, nrf, 12 mai 1953, 280pp.
With an introduction by Véra Daumal (see Bb56). Contains Ab6.3 (under title 'Sur *L'Ame primitive*'), Ab6.4, Ab13, Ab14.7, Ab18 (under title 'La Poésie et la Critique'), Ab33.1, Ab49, Ab66, Ab67.1, Ab67.3, Ab68, Ab83, Ab90, Ab91.1, Ab97, Ab98, Ab100, Ab101 (under title '*Hermès*, juill. 1937 [Bruxelles]'), Ab102.2, Ab111.1, Ab111.2, Ab112, Ab118, Ab119.1, Ab122, Ab129, Ab130, Ab132 (under title 'La Bhagavad-Gita'), another version of Ab133, Ab135, Ab161 (under title 'Réponses aux

questions de Luc Dietrich'), Ab163, Ab183 (under title 'Qui présente l'auteur sous un jour plus intime'). Previously unpublished:
.1 'RD (Résumé de sa vie)', 9-13. Repr. Ab360.
.2 'Le Nœud gordien', 17-24. Repr. Aa288.1.
.3 'Le Surréalisme et Le Grand Jeu', 50-52. Repr. At239, Ab269, Aa288, Ab308.
.4 'La Pataphysique et la révélation du rire', 53-55. Draft version of Ab17. Repr. Ab269.
.5 'Dictionnaires et Encyclopédies', 164-67. Repr. Aa287.
.6 *'La Nuit remue'*, 172-73.
.7 *'Le Dict de Padma'*, 189-92. Repr. Aa287.

Ab185   'Suite au *Contre Ciel*', in *Les Lettres Nouvelles*, 4 (juin 1953), 444-50.
Contains draft version of Aa99.5 under title 'Mémoire de mes morts...' and
.1 'Il vient des profondes cavernes...', 444-45. Repr. Aa193.
.2 'Oh! pourvu qu'il y ait un qui brille...', 445. Repr. Aa193.
.3 'La lutte est sûre...', 447. Repr. Aa193.
.4 'L'homme pagaie vers les sources...', 448. Repr. Aa193, Ab253.
.5 'Pour chanter du matin au soir', 449-50. Repr. Aa193.
.6 'Les Déceptions', 450. Repr. Aa193.

Aa186   *Le Catéchisme*. Collège de Pataphysique, col. 'Ha-Ha', no.4, 80 E.P. [1953], 30pp (unpaginated), 333 copies. With the indication 'écrit par RD en 1935'.
Repr. Ab247, Aa248, At251, Aa287.

1954

RENE DAUMAL

Ab187   'Textes', in *CdS*, no.sp. 'Il y a dix ans RD', XXXVIII, 322 (mars 1954).
Contains articles and a bio-bibliography (see Ba73) and
.1 'Le Mensonge de la vérité', 363-66. Repr. At251, Aa287.
In section 'Poèmes' (367-73) there is Ab30.2 and the following, with the indication 'ces poèmes font partie d'un recueil *Poésie Noire, Poésie Blanche*, à paraître prochainement chez Gallimard':
.2 'Cruautés', 367. Repr. Aa193.
.3 'Une voix peu connue', 369. Repr. Aa193.
.4 'Le Seul', 370-72. Repr. Aa193, Aa271, At295.
.5 'Discours du pavé', 373. From ch.5 of Ab202. Repr. Aa193.
In section 'Lettres à Jean Ballard (extraits)' (374-80), letters

.6 Dated 23 juill. 1941 (extract), 374.
.7 Dated 8 oct. 1942 (extract), 375.
.8 Dated 16 nov. 1942 (extract), 375-76.
.9 Dated 6 jan. 1943 (extract), 376.
.10 Dated 30 avr. 1943 (extract), 377-78.
.11 Dated 20 jan. 1944 (extract), 378-80. Abr. version in Ab235.
Full version in Ab363.
In section 'Lettres à Jacques Masui' (393-404), letters
.12 Dated 9 juin 1941 (extracts), 393-94.
.13 Dated 29 juin 1941 (extracts), 394-95.
.14 Dated 8 août 1941 (extracts), 396-98. Repr. with slightly
different extracts in At284.
.15 Dated 2 oct. 1941 (extracts), 398-400. Repr. slightly
abbreviated in At284.
.16 Dated 14 avr. 1942 (extracts), 401-03.
.17 Dated 31 juill. 1942 (extracts), 403-04.

As188   'Traductions', ibid., 387-90.
.1 *Bhagavad-Gita*, xv', 387-90. Repr. Aa265, Aa271.
.2 'Lois de Manou (Ch.II) [*Mânavadharmaçastra*]', 391-92.
Repr. Aa265.

Ab189   'Le Grand Magicien', *Les Lettres Nouvelles*, 14 (avr. 1954),
535-37.
Repr. At251, Aa287.

Ae190   Ae153 in a new collective edition , same title, with indication
'traduits sous la direction de Jean Herbert. Préface de J. Bacot.
Première série (Troisième édition, augmentée d'un index)'.
Albin Michel, coll. 'Spiritualités vivantes', 'série Bouddhisme',
juin 1954, 512pp.
(RD's translation of original vol.2 is on 291-482.)

Ab191   'Poèmes', in *NRF*, IV, 22 (1 août 1954), 246-49.
.1 'Je n'ai pas pu savoir...', 246. Repr. Aa193.
.2 'L'Abandon', 247. Repr. Aa193, Aa271.
.3 'Cave des cœurs...', 248. Repr. Aa193.
.4 'Madame Minuit...', 248. Repr. Aa193.
.5 'Origine de l'astronomie', 249. Repr. Aa193, Aa213.154.
.6 'Les Quatre temps cardinaux', 249. Repr. Aa193, Aa271.

Ab192   Extracts from Ab66 in *Pour l'Art* [Lausanne], 38 (sept.-oct. 1954),
26-27.
Accompanies article 'La rythmique, porte ouverte sur les arts',
by Madeleine Chabloz.

Aa193   *Poésie noire, poésie blanche. Poèmes.* Gallimard, nrf,
14 oct.1954, 254pp. With an introduction by V[éra] D[aumal]
(see Bb82).
Contains Ab3, Ab6.2, Ab8.1, Ab8.2, Ab14.3, Ab14.4, Ab14.5,
Ab14.6, Ab28, Ab29.1, Ab29.2, Ab29.3, Ab29.4, Ab29.5, Ab29.6,
Ab29.7, Ab29.8, Ab29.9, Ab30.1, Ab30.2, Ab33.2, Ab42.1,
Ab42.2, Ab42.3, Ab42.4, Ab43, Ab44, Ab55, Ab86 (without
title), Aa99.1, Aa99.2, Aa99.3, Aa99.4, Aa99.5, Aa99.6, Aa99.7,
Aa99.8, Aa99.9, Aa99.10, Aa99.11, Aa99.12, Aa99.13, Aa99.14,
Ab113, Ab126, Ab141, Ab169 (under title 'Le Père Mot'),
Ab185.1, Ab185.2, Ab185.3, Ab185.4, Ab185.5, Ab185.6,
Ab187.2, Ab187.3, Ab187.4, Ab187.5, Ab191.1, Ab191.2,
Ab191.3, Ab191.4, Ab191.5, Ab191.6. Previously unpublished:
.1 'Lettre à une bergère', 89-90.
.2 'Devant tout un peuple assemblé...', 91.
.3 'Le Raccommodeur de monstres', 92-93.
.4 'La peau de lumière vêtant ce monde...', 94.
.5 'Récit lamentable', 95-96.
.6 'Le Rire mort', 97.
.7 'Tourne-tue', 99-100.
.8 'La Chair de terreur', 101.
.9 'Retour au pays mauvais', 107.
.10 'Poème pour désosser les philosophes intitulé "L'au-delà
    misérable"', 112-15. Repr. Aa271.
.11 'Sorcellerie', 125. Repr. Aa271.
.12 'La Nuit derrière la nuit', 126.
.13 'Palais hippogriffe', 127.
.14 'La Consolatrice', 128. Repr. Aa271.
.15 'L'Autre Abandon', 133-34. Repr. Aa271, At295.
.16 'L'Etouffoir', 138-39. Repr. Aa271.
.17 'Fièvre blanche', 142-43. Repr. Aa271.
.18 'Jour, ô scandale', 144-45. Repr. Aa271.
.19 'Naufrage de nuit', 146. Repr. Aa271, At295.
.20 'La Sueur panique', 149-50. Repr. Aa271.
.21 'Creux de songe', 152. Repr. Aa271.
.22 'La Mère-mensonge', 157-58. Repr. Aa271.
.23 'Morale', 159. Repr. Aa271.
.24 'L'Hiver fait monter les fourmis', 160.
.25 'Le Fond du sort', 161-62. Repr. Aa271.
.26 'La Dernière Race', 163-65. Repr. Aa271.
.27 'Exactement à deux doigts de la mort', 167-68. Repr.
    Aa271.
.28 'Défi', 169. Repr. Aa271.
.29 'Le Pays des métamorphoses', 170-71. Repr. Aa271.
.30 'La Pierre lucide', 172. Repr. Aa271, At295.
.31 'O lent coureur la mort au cœur...', 186-87.

.32 'La grande transmutation qui change la face...', 190.
.33 'Il y a encore des lois mathématiques...', 192.
.34 'Si d'une impitoyable courbe...', 193.
.35 'Chanson réaliste', 203-04. Repr. Ab253.
.36 'Grand premier couple oscillant du ciel...', 225-26.
.37 'Un chœur pendulaire se dit et se contredit...', 227-28.
Also contains a number of prose works. Previously published: extract from Aa116 (part 3, ch. 3, the invocation to the sun); Ab119.2; extracts from Aa180 (ch.1, last paragraph; ch.4, the myth of 'La Sphère et la Tétrahèdre'); Aa180.4; Ab187.5, and two extracts from a previously unpublished prose work:
.38 'Au cœur de la nuit brille l'anti-lueur...', 197-98. Extract from Ab202, ch.5, part 12.
.39 'Nouveau discours du pavé', 201-02. Extract from Ab202, ch.5, part 10.

Aa194 Reprint of Aa155, nov. 1954, 157pp.

Ab195 'Correspondance avec RD', in *Cahiers du Collège de Pataphysique*, 8-9 (80 E.P.[1954]), 45-52.
Contains anonymously annotated (see Bb86) letters to Julien Torma,
.1 Dated vendredi 11 [déc. 1925], 45-46. Repr. Aa213.
.2 Undated fragment, 48. Repr. Aa213.
.3 Undated, 49-50. Repr. Aa213.
Pierre Minet considers these letters to be apocryphal (see Bb253).

ROGER GILBERT-LECOMTE

Ab196 'Quatre rêves', in *NRF*, III, 15 (1 mars 1954), 456-61. With notes by Arthur Adamov (see Bb75).
Contains Ab177 and
.1 'Arsenal', 457-58. Repr. Aa205, Aa319.
.2 'L'Oiseau la mort', 458-59. Repr. Aa205, Aa319.
.3 'Les Arguties de la conscience du rêve. La paralysie des côtes, l'engourdissement des membres', 459-60. Repr. Aa205, At318, Aa319.

1955

RENE DAUMAL

Ab197 Ab137 in *Qui est Lanza del Vasto? Etudes, témoignages, textes.* (Denoël, jan. 1955, 304pp.), 36-55.

Ab198   'Lettres à Max-Pol Fouchet', in *NRF*, V, 26 (1 fév. 1955),
        280-84.
        With an introduction by Véra Daumal (see Bb89). Contains letters
        .1 Dated 2 nov. 1940, 280-81.
        .2 Dated 8 mars 1941 (extracts), 281-84. Fragments repr.
        Aa261, At284.

Ae199   New edition of Ae174, mai 1955.

Ac200   'Entretiens sur divers sujets par Joë Bousquet, RD, Carlo
        Suarès', *Les Lettres Nouvelles*, 31 (oct. 1955), 429-45.
        Repr. Ac204.

Ab201   Ab29.8 in *Reflets* [Lyon] (nov. 1955), 17.

Ab202   'Traité des patagrammes', *Cahiers du Collège de Pataphysique*,
        16 (82 E.P. [1955]), 3-26.
        With an introduction by J.-H. Sainmont (see Bb116). Contains
        Ab183, Aa193.38, Aa193.39. Repr. Aa213 (section 11), Aa288.

Ab203   'Bubu-Magazine (numéro spécimen & numéro deux)', *Cahiers
        du Collège de Pataphysique*, 25 (84 E.P. [1955]), 7-11.
        With the indication 'les deux livraisons (manuscrites), que nous
        publions intégralement, ont été conservées dans les papiers
        de RD et sont entièrement écrites de sa main'.

Ac204   'Les Paralipomènes de *La Comédie Psychologique*', in Carlo
        Suarès, *Critique de la Raison Impure et les paralipomènes
        de La Comédie Psychologique composés sous forme de dialogues
        avec Joë Bousquet et RD (Textes inédits)* (Stock [Bruxelles],
        1955, 312pp.), 11-84.
        11-31 previously published as Ac200.

ROGER GILBERT-LECOMTE

Aa205   *Testament. Poèmes et textes en prose. Introduction d'Arthur
        Adamov. Avant-propos de Pierre Minet* (see Bb101). Gallimard,
        nrf, coll. 'Métamorphoses', no. 50, août 1955, 155pp.,
        1500 copies.
        Contains a bibliography (19) and six sections:
        [Section 1:] *Poèmes*. Contains Aa61.2, Aa61.11, Aa61.12,
        Aa61.19, Aa61.32, Aa104.3, Aa104.4, Aa104.5, Aa104.6,
        Aa104.7, Ab159.1, Ab159.2, Ab162.1 and
        .1 'Chassé-croisé du coma', 41. Repr. Aa319.

.2 'Hommage fraternel ou La Bête immonde', 52-54. Repr. Aa319.

.3 'Au vent du nord', 58. Repr. Aa319.

[Section 2:] *Rêves*. Contains Ab177, Ab196.1, Ab196.2, Ab196.3 and

.4 'Rêve de mort [A la sortie du banquet...]', 72. Repr. At318, Aa319.

.5 'Rêve à combler', 73. Repr. Aa319.

[Section 3:] *Essais* [*sic*]. Contains Ab123.

[Section 4:] *Fragments*. Contains Ab162.2 (under title 'Acte de dépossession (Tension)'), Ab162.3 (under title 'Oui et non. Raison-système-choc du chaos'), Ab166.1, a more complete version of Ab166.2, Ab168.1, Ab168.2, Ab168.3, Ab168.4, Ab168.5, Ab171.2, Ab171.4, Ab171.5 and

.6 'Et le devoir de créer...', 96. Repr. Aa301 [175].

.7 'A la chance fragile...', 97. Repr. Aa301 [175].

.8 'Parmi le ressac des larmes...', 102. Repr. Aa301 [177-78].

.9 'Complainte du ludion', 103. Repr. At318, Aa319 [161-62].

.10 'Carnet de route d'un trépassé', 104-06. Repr. Aa315, Aa319 [159-161].

.11 'Le Rite obscur du mythe souterrain', 107-08. Repr. Aa319 [202-03].

[Section 5:] *Notes diverses*. Contains Ab168.3, Ab168.4, Ab168.5, Ab171.3, Ab171.6, Ab171.7, Ab171.8, and

.12 'Il n'y a pas deux moyens...', 119. Repr. Aa301 [172].

.13 'Je crois au tragique...', 119. Repr. Aa301 [172].

.14 'Des mots humains...', 119. Repr. Aa301 [172].

.15 'Dans le désert mental...', 119-20. Repr. Aa301 [172].

.16 'Vous me faites danser...', 120. Repr. Aa301 [173].

.17 'L'intérieur du masque...', 120. Repr. Aa301 [173].

.18 'Je voudrais connaître...', 120. Repr. Aa296, Aa301 [170].

.19 'Les phosphènes...', 120. Repr. Aa296, Aa301 [170].

.20 'J'apporte une vérité monotone...', 121. Repr. Aa301 [173].

.21 'Le livre dont les feuilles...', 121. Repr. Aa296, Aa301 [170].

.22 'Comparer deux objets...', 121. Repr. Aa301 [173].

.23 'La terre et l'eau...', 121. Repr. Aa301 [173].

.24 'Le palais rouge...', 122. Repr. Aa296, Aa301 [170].

.25 'La vraie vie...', 123-24. Repr. Aa301.38 [270].

.26 'Mon admiration...', 124. Incorporates a fragment of Ab134. Repr. Aa301.38 [270].

.27 'Freud − méthode ascétique...', 124.

.28 'Ecrivant peu...', 125. Repr. Aa301 [228; to 'l'essentiel'].

.29 'J'ai déjà tenté...', 125. Repr. Aa301 [228; to 'dans l'erreur'].

.30 'Ma prédestination...', 125. Repr. Aa301 [229; variant of note beginning 'Pourquoi parler...'].

[Section 6:] *Retour à tout (Projets de préface, notes).* Contains Ab162.5, Ab162.6 (abr.), Ab162.7 and the following:

.31 'L'Efficacité de l'œuvre', 129. Repr. Aa301 [166].

.32 'Retour à tout − Fin de l'ère chrétienne. Naissance du troisième homme', 130-33. Repr. Aa301 [221-23].

.33 'Vocabulaire', 134-35. Repr. Aa301 [224].

.34 'Le Double Hermétisme', 136. Repr. Aa301 [224-25].

.35 'J'ai l'absolu certitude...', 137. Repr. Aa301 [227].

.36 'La Nature de la conscience vivante', 138. Repr. Aa301 [200].

.37 'La Connaissance mythique', 139-40. Repr. Aa301 [231].

.38 'La Révélation de la troisième heure', 145-46. Repr. Aa301 [231-32, where this and the previous entry are combined according to the original typescript].

.39 'Refus d'obéissance', 147. Repr. Aa301 [248].

.40 'Psychologie des états', 148. More complete version repr. Aa301 [195].

.41 'Métaphysique de l'absence', 149-50. More complete version repr. Aa301 [198].

1956

RENE DAUMAL

Ae206 Ae154 and Ae165 in a collective edition, *traduits sous la direction de Jean Herbert. Deuxième série (Troisième édition augmentée d'un index).* Albin Michel, coll. 'Spiritualités vivantes', 'série Bouddhisme', juin 1956, 942pp.
(RD's translation of the original volumes 3 & 4 are on 519-764 & 765-918 respectively.)

1957

RENE DAUMAL

Ab207 'Lettres', in *NRF*, IX, 50 (1 fév. 1957), 269-82.
Correspondence with RGL (see also Ab209). With an introduction by Véra Daumal (see Bb129). Contains letters to

.1 RGL and Meyrat, Robert, dated 1926, 276-80. Repr. Aa213, Ab269.

.2 RGL dated 1928, 280-82. Repr. Aa213 where it is dated [1927 ou 1928]. This letter also contains a poem:

.3 'Le vent donne soif aux chasseurs...', 282. Repr. Aa213.67.

Aa208   *Petit Théâtre*. Collège de Pataphysique, coll. 'Ha-Ha', no.11,
84 E.P. [1957], 44pp., 580 copies.
In collaboration with RGL (see Aa211). Introduction by J.-H.
Sainmont (see Bb132).
.1 'En Gggarrrde! Petit drame', 28-38.
.2 'Chronique médicale', 39-43.

ROGER GILBERT-LECOMTE

Ab209   'Lettres', in *NRF*, IX, 50 (1 fév. 1957), 269-82.
Correspondence with RD. With an introduction by Véra Daumal
(see Bb129). Contains letters
.1 Dated 17 sept. 1923, 269-74. Repr. Aa280 where it is wrongly
addressed to Roger Vailland.
.2 Dated 17 fév. 1927, 274-76. Repr. Aa280.

Ab210   'Tétanos mystique', *CdS*, XLIV, 340 (avr. 1957), 392-95.
Repr. Aa292, Aa319.

Aa211   *Petit Théâtre*. Collège de Pataphysique, coll. 'Ha-Ha', no.11,
84 E.P. [1957], 44pp., 580 copies.
In collaboration with RD. Introduction by J.-H. Sainmont
(see Bb132).
.1 'L'Odyssée d'Ulysse le Palmipède', 13-18. Repr. Aa319.
.2 'Conte', 19-22. Repr. Aa319.
.3 'Amour, amour!', 23-27. Repr. Aa319.

1958

RENE DAUMAL

As212   As92 (without the notes) in *Les Cahiers de la Compagnie Renaud-
Barrault*, 22-23 (mai 1958), 81-96.

Aa213   *Lettres à ses amis I*. Gallimard, nrf, 11 sept. 1958, 376pp.
Introduction by Véra Daumal-Page (see Bb138). Contains
13 sections:
[Section 1:] *Aux parents (1915-1926)*; letters to
.1   Mother dated 8 mars 1915, 9.
.2   Father dated [1915], 9-10.
.3   Mother dated [1915], 10. FMS on 11.
.4   Mother dated 10 juin 1918, 10.
.5   Father dated 15 juin 1918, 13.
.6   Father dated 23 juin 1918, 14. FMS (abr.) on 15.

.7   Parents dated 27 juin 1918, 14-16.
.8   Parents dated 14 juill. 1918, 16.
.9   Parents dated 18 juill. 1918, 16-17.
.10 Parents dated 21 juill. 1918, 17.
.11 Parents dated 26 juill. 1918, 18.
.12 Parents dated 28 juill. 1918, 18-19.
.13 Parents dated 1 août 1918, 19.
.14 Parents dated 4 août 1918, 19-20.
.15 Parents dated [1925], 20-21.
.16 Parents dated 8 nov. [1925], 21-22.
.17 Parents dated [1925], 23.
.18 Parents dated [1925], 24.
.19 Parents dated [1925] (postcard), 24-25.
.20 Parents dated [1925] (postcard), 25.
.21 Parents dated [1925] (postcard), 26.
.22 Parents dated jan. [1926], 26-27.
.23 Parents dated 13 jan. 1926, 28.
.24 Parents dated 1 fév. [1926], 28-29.
.25 Parents dated 5 mars 1926, 29-30.
.26 Parents dated 13 avr. 1926, 30-31.
.27 Parents dated 19 avr. [1926], 31.
.28 Parents dated 27 jan. 1926, 31-32.
.29 Parents dated [1926], 32-33.
.30 Parents dated mai 1926, 33-34.
.31 Parents dated [1926], 34-35.
.32 Parents dated 18 oct. 1926, 35-36.
.33 Parents dated [1926], 36-38.
.34 Parents dated [1926], 38.
.35 Parents dated 6 déc. [1926], 38-39.
[Section 2:] *A Roger Vailland (1925-1927)*:
.36 Dated [1925], 40-42.
.37 Dated [1925], 43-45.
.38 Dated [1925], 46-47.
.39 Dated [1925], 47-52.
.40 Dated [1925], 52-55.
.41 Dated 22 août 1925, 55-58.
.42 Dated [1925], 58-61.
.43 Dated [1926], 61-62.
.44 Dated [1925 ou 1926], 62-63.
.45 Dated [1927], 63-67.
[Section 3:] *A RGL (1925-1927)*. Contains Ab207.1, Ab207.2. The latter contains a different poem than previously published:
.46 'En suivant le chemin des gustaves...', 118-19.
The section contains letters to RGL (except where otherwise indicated)
.47 Dated [1925], 68-75.

50

.48 Dated [1926], 75-76.
.49 Dated [3 fév. 1926], 80-83.
.50 Dated [1927], 83-84.
.51 Dated [1927], 84-86.
.52 Dated 15 sept. 1927, 86.
.53 Dated [1927], 86-87.
.54 'Mes yeux sont tendus...', transcription of dream dated 18 mai 1927, wrongly described as a letter, 87-88.
.55 Dated [1927], 89.
.56 Letter to Rolland de Renéville, André, dated [1927], 89-91. Wrongly addressed to RGL; repr. Aa261 where Jack Daumal points out the error of addressee.
.57 Dated [1927], 91-92. Extract repr. Ab242.
.58 Dated [1927], 92-93.
.59 Dated [1927], 93.
.60 Dated [1927], 94-96.
.61 Dated [1927], 97-98.
.62 Dated [1927], 98-101.
.63 Dated [1927 ou 1928], 101-02.
.64 Dated [1928], 102-03.
.65 Dated [1928], 103-04.
.66 Dated [1928], 104-06.
.67 Dated [1928], 106-08. Contains Ab207.3. Extract repr. Ab242.
.68 Dated [1928] (postcard), 108.
.69 'On n'aime que ce qu'on n'a pas...', prose text wrongly described as a letter, 109-10.
.70 Dated [1928], 110-11.
.71 Dated [1928], 111-12.
.72 Dated 13-14 nov.(?) [1928], 112-15.
.73 Dated [1928], 119.
.74 Dated [1929], 120-22.
[Section 4:] *A Richard Weiner (1927)*:
.75 Dated [1927], 123.
.76 Dated [1927], 123-24.
.77 Dated [1927], 124.
.78 Dated [1927], 125.
.79 Dated [1927], 125-26.
.80 Dated 8 août [1927], 126-27.
.81 Dated [1927], 127.
.82 Dated [1927], 128.
.83 Dated [1927], 129-30.
.84 Dated [1927], 130.
.85 Dated [1927], 130-31.
.86 Dated [1927], 131-32.
.87 Dated [1927], 132-33.

[Section 5:] *A Julien Torma (1925-1929)* contains Ab195.1, Ab195.2, Ab195.3.

[Section 6:] *A Maurice Henry (1926-1930)*:
.88 Dated 8 juin 1926, 138-41.
.89 Dated juin 1927, 141-42.
.90 Dated 1928, 142-45. Extract repr. Ab242.
.91 Dated juill. 1928, 145-48.
.92 Dated [1929], 148-52.
.93 Dated 12 mars [1929], 153-57.
.94 Dated [1930], 158-65.

[Section 7:] *A A. Rolland de Renéville (1928-1930)* contains Ab33.3, and letters
.95 Dated 9 sept. 1928, 166.
.96 Dated 19 sept. 1928, 167-68.
.97 Dated 24 oct. 1928, 168-69.
.98 Dated 20 nov. 1928, 169-70.
.99 Dated 13 jan. 1929, 170-71.
.100 Dated 20 mai 1929, 171-72.
.101 Dated 2 juin 1929, 172.
.102 Dated 17 juill. 1929, 173-74.
.103 Dated 2 nov. 1929, 174-75.
.104 Dated 1 avr. 1930, 175-78.
.105 Dated 8 avr. 1930, 178-80.
.106 Dated 26 avr. 1930, 180-84.
.107 Dated 12 mai 1930, 184-85.
.108 Dated 3 juin 1930, 185-87.
.109 Dated 13 [juin 1930], 187-97. Contains Ab33.3.
.110 Dated 14 juin 1930, 197-98.
.111 Dated [juin 1930], 198-201. Contains As215.1, As215.2, As215.3, As215.4.
.112 Dated 26 juin 1930, 201-03. Contains Ac214.
.113 Dated 7 juill. 1930, 203-04.
.114 Dated 3 août 1930, 204-05.
.115 Dated 9 sept. 1930, 205-07.
.116 Dated 17 sept. 1930, 207-10. Last paragraph repr. Aa261.
.117 Dated 21 sept. 1930, 210-11.
.118 Dated 29 sept. 1930, 211-13.
.119 Dated 3 nov. 1930, 214-19.
.120 Dated 9 nov. 1930, 220-23.
.121 Dated 21 déc. 1930, 223-26.

[Section 8] *A Hendrick Cramer (1929-1930)*:
.122 Dated 12 oct. [1929], 227-29.
.123 Dated 6 jan. 1930, 229-31. Contains As215.1, As215.2, As215.3, As215.4.
.124 Dated 31 jan. 1930, 231-33.
.125 Dated 21 mars 1930, 233-34.

.126 Dated [juin 1930], 234-37. Same as Aa213.111.
.127 To Milanova, Véra, & Cramer, Hendrick, dated 12 oct.
[1929], 237-38.
[Section 9:] *A Véra Milanova (1928-31)*:
.128 Dated 30 déc. 1928, 241-43.
.129 Dated 6 mai 1929, 243-44.
.130 Dated 23 mai 1929, 245-47.
.131 Dated 12 oct. 1929, 247-48.
.132 Dated 5-6 nov. 1929, 248-49.
.133 Dated 21 mars 1930, 249-50.
.134 Dated 25 mai 1930, 251-52.
.135 Dated 8 juin 1930, 253-55.
.136 Dated 21 oct. 1930, 256-58.
.137 Dated 9 ou 10 nov. 1930, 259-60.
.138 Dated 22 jan. 1931, 260-63.
.139 Dated 26 mai 1931, 263-65.
[Section 10:] *A A. Rolland de Renéville (1931-32)*:
.140 Dated 16 avr. 1931, 266-68.
.141 Dated 2 sept. 1931, 268-71.
.142 Dated 15 sept. 1931, 272-78.
.143 Dated 22 sept. 1931, 279-89.
.144 Dated 10 nov. 1931, 289-92.
.145 Dated 12 oct. 1931, 292-93.
.146 Dated [1931], 293-94.
.147 Dated 10 jan. 1932, 294-96.
.148 Dated 26 jan. 1932 (postcard), 296.
.149 Dated [1932], 297-301.
.150 Dated 8 fév. 1932, 301-03.
.151 Dated [1932], 303-07.
.152 Dated 24 (?) juill. [1932], 307-10. Contains a poem:
.153 'Rêverie', 309.
.154 Dated [1932], 310-18. Contains Ab191.5.
.155 Dated 3 mars 1932, 318-26.
.156 Dated 1 avr. 1932, 326-27.
.157 Dated 1 oct. [1932], 327-29.
.158 Dated 2 déc. 1932, 330.
[Section 11:] *A Artür Harfaux (1932)*. Contains Ab183, Aa193.38,
Aa193.39, Ab202.
[Section 12:] *A André Suarès (1932)*. Contains Ab50.1.
[Section 13:] *A Jean Paulhan (1932)*. Contains
.159 Letter to Paulhan, Jean, dated [1932], 371-74.

Ac214   Letter to Tagore, Rabindranath, dated 26 juin 1930, ibid., 202-03.
Drafted by André Delons; RD & RGL are co-signatories. Repr.
Aa261, A269.

As215 Fragments, ibid.
.1 Unidentified fragment, 198-201. Repr. 234-37 of this volume and Ab240, Ab294.
.2 *'Shvetashvatara Upanishad IV, 3, 4'*, 230-31.
.3 *'Taittirîya Upanishad, Vallî III, 10'*, 231.
.4 *'Shukla Yajur Vêda, Shânti-pâtha'*, 231.

Ae216 Ae108 in a new edition, Club des Libraires de France, 1958, 225pp.

ROGER GILBERT-LECOMTE

Ac217 Letter to Tagore, Rabindranath, dated 26 juin 1930, in Aa213, 202-03.
Drafted by André Delons; RD & RGL are co-signatories. Repr. Ab264, Ab275.

1959

RENE DAUMAL

At218 *Mount Analogue. An Authentic Narrative.* Translation and intro-duction by Roger Shattuck; with a postface by Véra Daumal (see Bb152). Vincent Stuart Ltd [London], 1959, 106pp.
Translation of Aa180. Repr. At219, At249, At369.

1960

RENE DAUMAL

At219 Same as At218 but with sub-title *A Novel of Symbolically Authentic Non-Euclidean Adventures in Mountain Climbing.* Pantheon [New York], 1960, 160pp. Repr. 370.

ROGER GILBERT-LECOMTE

Aa220 *Sacre et massacre de l'amour.* Same as Aa61.19 in *Joseph Sima,* Paul Fachetti, 10 déc. 1960, 48pp. (unpag.), 160 copies.
Accompanies 8 original lithographs by Sima.

1961

RENE DAUMAL

At220a   Claviculas de un gran juego poético.
Probably a translation of Aa99.1 by Aquiles Ferrario. Fabril [Buenos Aires], 1961. With an introduction (see Bb160b).

At220b   El Monte Análogo.
Translation of Aa180 by Alicia Renard, Mundonuevo [Buenos Aires], 1961.

1962

RENE DAUMAL

Aa221   New edition of Aa180. Gallimard, 15 mars 1962, 216pp.

ROGER GILBERT-LECOMTE

Ab222   Ab39.2 [part] 1 in *NRF*, XX, 117 (1 sept. 1962), 567-76. With an introduction by Bruno Roy (see Bb167).

Ab223   Ab39.2 [part] II, in *NRF*, XX, 118 (1 oct. 1962), 761-68.

1963

RENE DAUMAL

Ab224   Ab43 in the catalogue of the exhibition *Joseph Sima à travers les collections rémoises*, Musée des Beaux-Arts de Reims [Reims], fév. 1963, 1p. (unpag.), 375 copies.

ROGER GILBERT-LECOMTE

Ab225   Ab24, ibid., 6pp. (unpag.).

Ab226   Ab41 in *NRF*, XXI, 122 (1 fév. 1963), 375-76.

1964

RENE DAUMAL

As227   'L'Hymne de l'Homme' [*Rig-Veda, IXe Mandala*]', *Hermès* [Bruxelles], 2 (hiver-print. 1964 [1er trim. 1964], 37-48. With an introduction by Jacques Masui (see Bb175). Repr. Aa265, At355.

Ae228   Ae108 in *Ernest Hemingway, Œuvres Complètes, IV. Lithographies originales de Pelayo.* André Sauret [Monte-Carlo], 27 avr. 1964, 384pp.

At229   *Der Analog. Ein Wahrheitsgetreuer Bericht.* Aa180 translated into German by Albrecht Fabri. Karl Rauch [Düsseldorf], 1964, 158pp. Repr. At353.

ROGER GILBERT-LECOMTE

Ab230   'Une lettre inédite de RGL [to Benjamin Fondane]', dated 22 mars 1933, *CdS*, LVII, 377 (mai-juin 1964), 388-94. Introduced by Claude Sernet (see Bb182). Repr. Ab327, Ab367.

1965

RENE DAUMAL

Ae231   Ae108 in new edition, Livre de Poche, no.1338-39, 4e trim. 1965, 512pp.

Ab232   Ab87 in *Les Cahiers de la Compagnie Renaud-Barrault*, 51 (nov. 1965), 9-11.

Aa233   *Le Lyon rouge suivi de Tempête de cygnes ou La Conquête des signes.* Collège de Pataphysique, coll. 'Ha-Ha', no.16, 91 E.P. [1965], 17pp., 777 copies. In collaboration with RGL. Repr. Ab277, Ac311.

ROGER GILBERT-LECOMTE

Aa234   *Le Lyon rouge suivi de Tempête de cygnes ou La Conquête*

des signes. Collège de Pataphysique, coll. 'Ha-Ha', no.16, 91 E.P. [1965], 17pp., 777 copies.
In collaboration with RD. Repr. Ac281, Aa319.

1966

RENE DAUMAL

Ab235   Previously published texts in Michel Random, *Les Puissances du Dedans*, Denoël, 19 sept. 1966, 448pp.
Contains Ab126, Ab139 (with the exception of the last four paragraphs), Ab141, Ab187.11 (with the exception of the first and last two paragraphs).

Ae236   Ae108 in *Ernest Hemingway, Œuvres romanesques, I.* Edited by Roger Asselineau (Gallimard, coll. 'Bibliothèque de la Pléiade', no. 189, 1966, 1476pp.), 985-1307.

ROGER GILBERT-LECOMTE

Aa237   *Monsieur Morphée, empoisonneur public.* Same as Ab26. Fata Morgana [Montpellier], 13 oct. 1966, 36pp. (unpag.), 332 copies. Frontispiece by Joseph Sima, introduction by Claude Sernet (see Bb192). Includes
         .1 Letter to Sernet, Claude, undated (FMS), 1p. (unpag.). Repr. Ab350.

1967

RENE DAUMAL

Ab238   Texts in *La Grive*, no. sp. 'RD', 135-36 (juill.-déc. 1967).
Contains articles on RD (see Ba199) and
         .1 'Fragments d'une lettre inédite à Jean Paulhan, dated 1 mai 1937', 4-5. Repr. Ab242 (abr.), Ab267 (extracts).
         .2 'Une lettre inédite de RD [to Luc Périn, dated 15 avr. 1943]', 20-21.
         .3 'RD et les Ardennes. Lettre inédite [dated 28 sept. 1943]', 24. A fake according to Guichard (see Ba481).

At239   *Il "Grand Jeu". Scritti di RGL e RD. Immagini di Joseph Sima.*
With an introduction by Claudio Rugafiori (see Bb200). Adelphi

[Milano], coll. 'Fascicoli', no.1, agosto 1967, xxiv & 274pp. Contains translations into Italian of Ab3, Ac5, Ab6.1, Ab6.2, Ab14.3, Ab14.4, Ab16, Ab17, Ab29.1, Ab29.2, Ab29.6, Ab29.7, Ab29.8, Ab33.1, Ab33.2, Ab33.3, Ab42.1, Ab42.2, Ab42.3, Ab42.4, Ab43, Aa99.5, Aa184.3.

Ab240   Texts in section 'Choix de textes' of Jean Biès, *RD* (Seghers, coll. 'Poètes d'aujourd'hui', no.169, 30 oct. 1967, 196pp.), 124-83.
Contains Ab55, Ab113, Ab119.2, Ab126, Ab131, Ab141, As215.1 and extracts from Ab14.7, Ab33.3, Aa116, Ab119.1, Ab163, Aa180 (includes a draft FMS), Aa180.4.

As241   'Rig-Véda (IXe cycle. Hymne 15: 'L'Offrande de la Liqueur')', ibid., 182-83.
Another version repr. As266.1. This version repr. Ab294, Ab345.

Ab242   Texts in *Hermès* [Bruxelles], no.sp. 'La Voie de RD, du *GJ* au *Mont Analogue*', 5 (1967-1968 [4e trim. 1967]).
Contains articles on RD (see Ba202), the following previously published texts by RD: Ac4 (under title 'La Circulaire du GJ'), Ac5; the following under section entitled 'Textes épars (Epoque du GJ) (1928-1934)': Ab14.2, Ab14.6 (abr.), Ab74, Ab76 and extracts from Ab6.1, Ab33.1, Ab50.2, Ab163, Aa213.57, Aa213.67, Aa213.90, Ab238.1. Previously unpublished letters to
.1 Rolland de Renéville, André, dated 6 sept. 1934 (extract), 48-50.
.2 Paulhan, Jean, dated 1935 (extract), 50.
.3 Paulhan, Jean, dated 6 juill. 1937 (extract), 50-51.
.4 Paulhan, Jean, dated 1935 (extract), 51.

As243   'Textes sanskrits traduits par RD', ibid., 76-86.
.1 *'Les Lois de Manou*, ch.IV, vers la fin du 2me tiers [*Mânavadharmaçastra*]', 77-81. Includes FMS of RD's transcription of the Sanskrit text and FMS of his notes. Repr. Aa265.
.2 *'Chândogya Upanishad*. Septième cycle. Les quatre premières sections', 81-83. Repr. Aa265.
.3 *'Rig-Véda (La Vision-des-Stances)*. 9e cycle. Hymne LXIX: Au Liquide', 84-86. Includes extracts from notes to the text. Repr. Aa265, Aa271, At355.

Aa244   Aa116, new edition, Gallimard, nov. 1967, 216pp.

Primary Material

ROGER GILBERT-LECOMTE

At245   *Il "Grand Jeu". Scritti di RGL e RD. Immagini di Joseph Sima.* With an introduction by Claudio Rugafiori (see Bb200). Adelphi [Milano], coll. 'Fascicoli', no.1, agosto 1967, xxiv & 274pp. Contains translations into Italian of Ab11, Ab12.1, Ab21, Ab22.1, Ab24, Ab26, Ab39.2, Ab41, Aa61.1, Aa61.19, Aa61.22, Aa61.23, Aa61.28, Aa61.29, Aa61.30, Aa61.31, Aa61.34, Aa61.37, Aa61.38.

Ab246   Texts in *Hermès* [Bruxelles], no.sp. 'La Voie de RD, du *GJ* au *Mont Analogue*', 5 (1967-1968 [4e trim. 1967]). Contains Ac10 (under title 'La Circulaire du GJ') and Ab11.

1968

RENE DAUMAL

Ab247   Aa186 in *La Grive*, 138 (avr.-juin 1968), 3-7. Illustrated with two drawings by Maurice Henry.

Aa248   *Le Catéchisme.* Same as Ab247, *tirage à part*, 8pp. (unpag.), 100 copies.

At249   Same as At218. City Lights Books [San Francisco], May 1968, 106pp.

At250   *Il Monte Analogo. Romanzo d'avventure alpine non Euclidee e simbolicamente autentiche.* Adelphi [Milano], coll. 'Biblioteca Adelphi', no. 19, luglio 1968, 186pp. Followed by a study by Claudio Rugafiori (see Bb225). Aa180 translated into Italian by Claudio Rugafiori.

At251   *I Poteri della Parola.* Adelphi [Milano], coll. 'Fascicoli', no. 4, luglio 1968, x & 238pp. Translated into Italian by Claudio Rugafiori. Introductions by Claudio Rugafiori and Jacques Masui (see Bb226). Contains translations of Ab67.1, Ab83, As85, Ab90, As92, Ab107, Ab119.1, Ab129, Ab135, Ab141, Ab152, Ab163, Ab169, Aa186, Ab187.1, Ab189.

Ab252   Aa180, new edition. Gallimard, 15 juill. 1968, 209pp. This edition repr. Aa290.

Ab253   'Deux poèmes de RD', *La Quinzaine Littéraire*, 56 (1 sept.
         1968), 4.
         Contains Ab185.4, Aa193.35 (without title).

Ab254   *Le Grand Jeu*. Minard, Cahiers de l'Herne, coll. 'L'écriture
         des vivants', no.2, 18 nov. 1968, 254pp.
         Edited by Marc Thivolet. Re-edition of the three issues of
         Le GJ, accompanied by articles, a chronology and a bibliography
         (see Ba239). Contains Ac4, Ac5, Ab6.1, Ab6.2, Ab6.3, Ab6.4,
         Ab9, Ab14.1, Ab14.2, Ab14.3, Ab14.4, Ab14.5, Ab14.6, Ab14.7,
         Ab14.8, Ac15.1, Ac15.2, Ac15.3, Ab29.8, Ac31 (without title),
         Ab33.1, Ab33.2, Ab33.3, Ab33.4, Ab33.5, Ac34.1. Previously
         unpublished:
         .1 'Projet de présentation du GJ', 17-18.
         In section entitled 'Textes inédits de RD' (203-24):
         .2 'Projet de sommaire du numéro 4', (extract), 204. Complete
            versions Ab269, Ab308.
         .3 'L'Asphyxie et l'expérience de l'absurde', 206-09. The table
            of contents has 'ou' for 'et'. Repr. Ab269, Aa288, Ab308,
            At347.
         .4 'Hegel, le pseudo-matérialisme et E. Meyerson', 210-16.
            Repr. Aa288, Ab308.
         .5 'Recherche de la nourriture', 217-28. Repr. Aa288.
         .6 'Les Petites Recettes du GJ', 219-21. Repr. Aa288.

ROGER GILBERT-LECOMTE

Ab255   Previously published texts in the catalogue to the exhibition
         of Sima's painting at the Musée National d'Art Moderne, Paris,
         7 Nov.-23 Dec. 1968.
         Catalogue published by the Centre National d'Art Contemporain,
         1968. Contains Ab24 (17-21) & Ab41 (23).

Ab256   *Le Grand Jeu*. Minard, Cahiers de l'Herne, coll. 'L'écriture des
         vivants', no.2, 18 nov. 1968, 254pp. Edited by Marc Thivolet.
         Re-edition of the three issues of *Le GJ*, accompanied by articles,
         a chronology and a bibliography (see Ba239). Contains Ac10,
         Ab11, Ab12.1, Ab12.2, Ab12.3, Ab22.1, Ab22.2, Ab22.3, Ab23.1,
         Ac23.2, Ac23.3, Ab37, Ab39.1, Ab39.2, Ab39.3, Ab39.4, Ab39.5,
         Ac40.

Ab257   'La Peinture de Joseph Sima', *Opus International*, 9 (déc. 1968),
         26-29. Repr. Aa301.

1969

RENE DAUMAL

Ab258   Texts in Jacques Masui, 'Poésie et négation chez RD', *Hermès*
[Bruxelles], no.sp. 'Le Vide. Expérience spirituelle en Occident et
en Orient', 6 ([1er trim. 1969]), 247-52.
  .1 'L'acte de nier...', 251.
  .2 Letter to Rolland de Renéville, André, undated (extract), 252.

Ab259   Ab126 in *Le Nouveau Planète*, 4 (fév. 1969), 53-57.
With an introduction by Louis Pauwels (see Bb254).

Aa260   Same as Aa116, Gallimard, 22 mai 1969, 216pp.

Aa261   *Tu t'es toujours trompé. Edition établie et présentée par Jack
Daumal.* Mercure de France, 30 déc. 1969 (copyright 1970), 256pp.
Unfinished draft essay written *circa* 1926-1928; 45-47 & 35-40
previously published in that order with minor modifications as
Ab17. The text is followed by a section entitled 'Documents'
(169-253) placing the essay in its context. These documents contain
extracts from previously published works: Ab58, Ab97, Aa180,
Ab198.2, Aa213.56 (with the correction of the addressee as André
Rolland de Renéville), Aa213.117, Ac214. Previously unpublished:
  .1 Letter to anon. dated 23 juin 1934 [ou 1935?], 203-07.
  .2 Letter to Dermenghem, Emile, dated 23 août 1934, 207-08.
  .3 'Esquisses du plan de l'ouvrage', 218-22.
  .4 'Notes diverses sur la Pataphysique', 223-27.
  .5 'L'Histoire du crocodile [FMS]', 228.

ROGER GILBERT-LECOMTE

Ab262   Ab26 in *Mandala. Essai sur l'expérience hallucinogène* (ed.
Jean-Claude Bailly & Jean-Pierre Guimard, Belfond, 25 juin 1969,
336pp.), 11-21.

Ab263   Texts in *NRF*, XXXIV, 203 (1 nov. 1969).
Under title 'Correspondance à Roger Vailland' (695-701) contains
letters to Roger Vailland
  .1 Undated, 695-97. Repr. Aa280.
  .2 Dated 13 mars 1927, 698-99. Repr. Aa280.
  .3 Dated sept. 1924, 699-701. Repr. Aa280.
Under title 'Poèmes' (718-25) contains:

   .4 'Les Dieux manchots', 718-20. Repr. Aa319.
   .5 'Non-titré [De nuit au poêle ensanglanté...]', 720-721.
   Repr. Aa319.
   .6 'Non-titré [Coq à crever ta gorge...]', 721. Repr. Aa319.
   .7 'Jamais, jamais le sang lumineux...', 721-22. Another
   version of Aa61.23. Repr. Aa319.
   .8 'Renaître prénatal', 722-24. Repr. Aa319 (abr.), Ab326.
   Complete version repr. Aa315, At372.
   .9 'Note pour la prophétie des rois-mages', 724. Repr.
   Aa301 [180].
  .10 'Le Grand Jeu en boitant...', 724-25. Repr. Aa301 [180].
  .11 'Holà, vice-roi...', 725. Repr. Aa301 [180-81].

Ab264   Texts in René Daumal, *Tu t'es toujours trompé. Edition établie et
présentée par Jack Daumal*. Mercure de France, 30 déc. 1969
(copyright 1970), 256pp. Contains Ac217 and
   .1 Letter to RD dated [1932] (extract), 198-99. Complete version
   repr. Aa280 where it is dated [1933].

1970

RENE DAUMAL

Aa265   *Bharata. L'Origine du théâtre. La Poésie et la musique en Inde.
Traductions de textes sacrés et profanes*. Gallimard, nrf, 4 fév.
1970, 211pp.
With an introduction by Jacques Masui (see Bb273) and an index.
Contains Ab48, As85, As92, Ab107, As128, Ab129, As188.1,
As188.2, As227, As243.1, As243.2, two versions of As243.3.
Previously unpublished:
   .1 'Réponse de RD à M. Boris de Schlœzer', 110-118. Draft
   version of Ab49.
   .2 'Préface', 119-21. Draft of a letter to Jean Paulhan, *circa*
   1942. FMS repr. Ab345. Also repr. At355.

As266   Translations from the Sanskrit, ibid.:
   .1 '*Rig-Véda*, 9e cycle: L'Offrande de la Liqueur', 138-39.
   Another version of As241. Repr. Ab345 (with FMS).
   .2 'Les Cinq Livres du Brahmane Vichnouçarman (*Pantcha-
Tantra*)', 155-200. Repr. At284 (also contains FMS). Another
   version of section 17bis repr. as part of As303.4.
Under title 'Fragments':
   .3 '[Viçanatha Kaviraja (fragment)]', 201-02.
   .4 '[Bhartrhari [III, 87] (fragment)]', 202. Repr. Ab345.

Ab267   Letters and extracts from letters (some previously published) in Michel Random, *Le Grand Jeu. 1. Essai* (Denoël, 15 sept. 1970). Contains Ab50.1 (238-39) and Ab238.1 (extracts, 88-89) and letters to
.1 Rolland de Renéville, André, dated 7 nov. 1929, 50-51.
.2 Rolland de Renéville, André, dated 28 jan. 1930 (extract), 53-54.
.3 Rolland de Renéville, André, dated 20 mars 1930, 57-60.
.4 Rolland de Renéville, André, dated 16 oct. 1931 (extracts), 69-70.
.5 Rolland de Renéville, André, dated 6 nov. 1931 (extract), 71.
.6 Paulhan, Jean, dated 16 août 1935 (extract), 87 (nota 2).

Ac268   Letter to Rolland de Renéville, André, dated 13 juill. 1929 (telegram).
In collaboration with RGL, ibid., 47. Repr. Ab269.

Ab269   Texts in Michel Random, *Le Grand Jeu. 2. Textes essentiels et documents* (Denoël, 15 sept. 1970). Contains Ac4, Ac5, Ab6.1, Ac15.1, Ac31, Ab33.3, Ab43, Ab58 (extracts), Ab163, Aa184.3, Aa184.4, Ab207.1, Ac214, complete version of Ab254.2 under title '*Le GJ*. No. 4. Sommaire', Ab254.3, Ac268. In section entitled 'La Dialectique de la révolte' (51-60), the following texts destined for *Le GJ* 4:
.1 'La Phénoménologie. Les Phénoménologistes et le GJ', 57-58. Repr. Ab308.
.2 'La Religion et le GJ', 58-59. Repr. Ab308, Ab324.

Ac270   'Plan et projet d'articles pour les numéros du *GJ*', ibid., 41-42. Probably written in collaboration with RGL.

Aa271   *Le Contre-Ciel suivi de Les Dernières Paroles de poète.* Gallimard, nrf, coll. 'Poésie', no. 63, 5 oct. 1970, 255pp.
With a preface (see Bb288.1) and a biography (see Bb288.2) by Claudio Rugafiori. Has four sections:
[Section 1:] *Le Contre-Ciel.* Same as Aa99.
[Section 2:] *Le Contre-Ciel (premier état).* Contains those poems which formed part of the first unpublished version: Ab3, Ab6.2, Ab8.1, Ab8.2, Ab14.3, Ab14.5, Ab28, Ab29.1, Ab29.2, Ab29.3, Ab29.4, Ab29.5, Ab29.6, Ab29.9, Ab30.1, Ab30.2, Ab33.2, Ab42.1, Ab42.2, Ab42.3, Ab42.4, Ab55, Ab187.4, Ab191.2, Aa193.10, Aa193.11, Aa193.14, Aa193.15, Aa193.16, Aa193.17, Aa193.18, Aa193.19, Aa193.20, Aa193.21, Aa193.22, Aa193.23, Aa193.25, Aa193.26, Aa193.27, Aa193.28, Aa193.29, Aa193.30.

The table of contents for this unpublished version is given 17-18.
[Section 3:] *Les Dernières paroles du poète*. Contains Ab113,
Ab126, Ab135, Ab141, Ab169 (under title 'Le Père Mot'),
Ab191.6.
[Section 4:] *Traductions du Sanskrit*. Contains As128 (under title
'La Connaissance de Soi'), As136 (without the final 'Notice'),
As188.1 (under title 'L'Etre actif suprême'), As243.3 (under
title 'Au liquide', and without the notes).
Also contains in the preface two previously unpublished
fragments:
.1 'Je veux vivre...', 7-8. Extract from ch.3 of Aa288.1.
.2 Letter to Paulhan, Jean, dated *circa* 1936 (extract), 16.
Errata for vol. in Ab345 on p.299.

At272   *La Gran Bevuta. Opere di RD a cura di Claudio Rugafiori, VI.*
Translation into Italian of Aa116 by Bianca Candian. Adelphi
[Milano], 1970, 220pp.

ROGER GILBERT-LECOMTE

Ab273   Letters and extracts from letters in Michel Random, *Le Grand
Jeu. 1. Essai* (Denoël, 15 sept. 1970) to
.1 Vailland, Roger, dated 3 jan. 1926 (extract), 31-32.
Complete version in Ab275 and Aa280.
.2 Vailland, Roger, dated 24 jan. 1926 (extract), 32.
Complete version in Aa280.
.3 Rolland de Renéville, André, dated 7 nov. 1929, 48-50.
.4 Puyaubert, Jean, dated [18 juin 1931] (extracts), 67-68.
Complete version in Aa280.
.5 RD dated 17 fév. 1931 (extract), 68. Complete version
in Aa280.
.6 RD dated mars 1932 (extract), 73-74. Complete version in
Aa280 where it is dated [1931].
.7 Henry, Maurice, dated 24 nov. 1942, 77.
.8 RD dated 28 juin 1932, 236-37. Repr. Aa280.

Ac274   Letter to Rolland de Renéville, André, dated 13 juill. 1929
(telegram).
In collaboration with RD, ibid., 47. Repr. Ab275.

Ab275   Texts in Michel Random, *Le Grand Jeu. 2. Textes essentiels et
documents* (Denoël, 15 sept. 1970).
Contains Ac10, Ab11, Ab12.1, Ab22.1, Ac23.1, Ab24, Ab37,
Ab41, Ac217, complete version of Ab273.1, Ac274, and

.1 Letter to Vailland, Roger, dated mai 1925 (extracts), 20-21. Complete version in Aa280.

.2 Letter to Vailland, Roger, and RD dated 13 mars 1926, 23-24. Repr. Aa280.

.3 Letter to Vailland, Roger, dated 1926 (extract), 24-26. Complete version in Aa280.

.4 'L'Activité de la conscience dans le rêve', 27-32.

The section entitled 'La Dialectique de la révolte' has the following texts destined for *Le GJ* 4:

.5 'La Dialectique de la révolte', 51-53. Abr. version repr. Ab317, Ab328, complete version Aa301.

.6 'Révolution-Révélation', 53-54. Repr. Aa301, Ab317.

.7 'La Psychanalyse', 54-57. Repr. Aa301, Ab317.

.8 'Les Chapelles littéraires modernes [II]', 111-23. Lecture delivered 19 nov. 1929. Repr. Aa301.

Ac276   'Plan et projet d'articles pour les numéros du *GJ*', ibid., 41-42. Probably written in collaboration with RD.

1971

RENE DAUMAL

Ab277   Texts in Jean-Michel Agasse, 'Poétique/Daumal' (Thèse de 3e cycle, Paris-Nanterre, juin 1971), vol.2. Contains Ab35, Ab84.1, Ab87, Ab96.3, Ab106, Ab139, Ab140, Ab142, Aa233, and the following letters to

.1 Anon. dated [1935?] (extract), 44-46.

.2 Paulhan, Jean, dated 3 juill. 1936, 47-49.

.3 Anon. dated [1938], 50-52.

Ab278   Texts in *La Grive* [Charleville-Mézières], XLIV, 152 (4e trim. 1971).

.1 'Dialectique de l'amour (diagram)', 24.

Under title 'Texte de RD':

.2 Letter to Paulhan, Jean, dated [1939], 29-31. Draft; contains a plan for a book entitled 'De l'obscurantisme moderne'. Repr. At284.

Ae279   Ae174 in new edition, 10 déc. 1971, 256pp. (117-223).

ROGER GILBERT-LECOMTE

Aa280   *Correspondance. Lettres adressées à RD, Roger Vailland,*

René Maublanc, Pierre Minet. Gallimard, nrf, 27 fév. 1971,
255pp. With a preface by Pierre Minet (see Bb320).
Contains Ab209.1, Ab209.2, Ab263.1, Ab263.2, Ab263.3, Ab273.8
Ab275.2, and the complete versions of the following partially
published letters: Ab264.1, Ab273.1, Ab273.2, Ab273.4, Ab273.5,
Ab273.6, Ab275.1, Ab275.3, and letters to
.1 Maublanc, René, dated 2 jan. 1923, 25.
.2 Maublanc, René, dated 11 jan. 1923, 25-26.
.3 Maublanc, René, dated 1 fév. 1923, 26.
.4 Maublanc, René, dated 10 fév. 1923, 27.
.5 Maublanc, René, dated 27 avr. 1923, 27-28.
.6 Maublanc, René, dated 29 août 1923, 28-29.
.7 Maublanc, René, dated 25 oct. 1923, 35.
.8 Maublanc, René, dated 16 jan. 1924, 35-36.
.9 Maublanc, René, dated 12 fév. 1924, 36.
.10 Maublanc, René, dated 26 fév. 1924, 36-37.
.11 Maublanc, René, dated 30 avr. 1924, 37-38.
.12 Maublanc, René, dated 20 juill. 1924, 38.
.13 Maublanc, René, dated 24 sept. 1924, 39-40.
.14 Maublanc, René, dated 25 jan. 1925, 44-45.
.15 Maublanc, René, dated 5 mars 1925, 45-46.
.16 Vailland, Roger, dated 25 avr. 2925 [*sic*], 46-47.
.17 Maublanc, René, dated 3 juill. 1925, 47-48.
.18 Vailland, Roger, dated 10 [août 1925], 48-50.
.19 Vailland, Roger, dated 12 août 1925, 51-55. Repr. Ab366.
.20 Maublanc, René, dated 18 août 1925, 55.
.21 Vailland, Roger, dated 2 sept. 1925, 56-62. Repr. Ab366.
.22 Vailland, Roger, dated 2 oct. 1925, 63-65.
.23 RD dated 7 oct. 2025 [*sic*], 66-69.
.24 Vailland, Roger, and RD dated oct. 1925, 70-73.
.25 Vailland, Roger, and RD dated 5 nov. 1925, 73-76.
.26 Vailland, Roger, dated 11 nov. 1925, 76-79.
.27 Vailland, Roger, dated 13 déc. 1925, 79-81.
.28 RD, undated, 81-84.
.29 RD and Vailland, Roger, dated [1925], 84-86.
.30 RD and Vailland, Roger, dated [1925], 89.
.31 Vailland, Roger, dated [1925], 90-93.
.32 Vailland, Roger, dated [1925], 93-95.
.33 Vailland, Roger, and RD dated [1925], 96-97.
.34 RD dated [1925], 97-99.
.35 Maublanc, René, dated 6 jan. 1926, 101.
.36 Maublanc, René, dated 2 fév. 1926, 104-05.
.37 Vailland, Roger, and RD dated 13 fév. 1926, 105-08.
.38 Vailland, Roger, and RD dated 19 mai 1926, 112-14.
.39 Vailland, Roger, and RD dated 2 juin 1926, 115-16.
.40 Vailland, Roger, and RD dated 13 juin 1926, 116-18.

.41 Vailland, Roger, and RD dated 5 juill. 1926, 119-20.
.42 Vailland, Roger, dated 6 juill. 1926, 121.
.43 Vailland, Roger, dated 21 août 1926, 122-23.
.44 Vailland, Roger, dated 8 sept. 1926, 123-27.
.45 Vailland, Roger, and RD dated 6 oct. 1926, 127-30.
.46 RD dated 9 oct. 1926, 130-33.
.47 RD and Vailland, Roger, dated 21 oct. 1926, 134.
.48 RD dated 30 oct. 1926, 135-36.
.49 Vailland, Roger, and RD dated 14 nov. 1926, 136-38.
.50 Vailland, Roger, and RD dated 26 nov. 1926, 138-39.
.51 Minet, Pierre, dated [1926], 146-48.
.52 Vailland, Roger, and RD dated [1926], 148-49.
.53 Vailland, Roger, Minet, Pierre, and RD dated [1926], 149-51.
.54 Vailland, Roger, and RD dated [1926], 151-53.
.55 RD dated 3 jan. 1927, 154-55.
.56 Maublanc, René, dated [7 juill. 1927], 159-60.
.57 Maublanc, René, dated 16 sept. 1927, 160.
.58 Maublanc, René, dated 11 oct. [1927], 161.
.59 RD dated 13 oct. 1927, 161-63.
.60 RD dated [1927], 164-65.
.61 Vailland, Roger, and RD dated [1927], 165-66.
.62 Vailland, Roger, and RD dated [1927], 166-67.
.63 RD dated [1927], 167-68.
.64 RD dated [1927], 169-70.
.65 RD dated [1927], 170-71.
.66 Vailland, Roger, and RD dated [1927], 171-72.
.67 Vailland, Roger, and RD dated [1927], 173-74.
.68 Vailland, Roger, and RD dated [1928], 174-75.
.69 RD dated [1928], 176-78.
.70 RD dated [1928], 179.
.71 RD dated [1928], 180-82.
.72 RD dated [1928], 183-84.
.73 RD dated [1928], 185-88.
.74 RD dated [1928], 188-89.
.75 RD dated 23 mai 1928, 190-91.
.76 Maublanc, René, dated 28 mai 1928, 191.
.77 RD dated [1928], 192.
.78 RD dated [1929], 193-94.
.79 RD dated 18 fév. 1930, 194-96.
.80 RD dated 23 avr. 1930, 196-98. Contains Aa61.25 and two more poems:
.81 'Absence de soleil...', 197. Repr. Aa319.
.82 'A forme et se saisit...', 198. Repr. Aa319.
.83 RD dated 28 avr. 1930, 198.
.84 RD dated [1931], 202-03.

.85 RD dated [1931], 205-07.
.86 RD dated 16 mars 1932, 210-11.
.87 Puyaubert, Jean, dated 22 mars 1932, 211-12.
.88 RD dated 24 mars 1932, 213-14.
.89 Milanova, Véra, dated 25 mai 1932, 214-15.
.90 RD dated 2 août 1932, 218-20.
.91 RD dated 1932, 221-22.
.92 RD dated 1932, 223.
.93 RD dated 11 août 1932, 224-25.
.94 RD dated 13 août 1932, 225-26.
.95 Puyaubert, Jean, dated 4 nov. 1932, 227.
.96 RD dated 17 nov. 1932, 228-29.
.97 Daumal, Véra, dated 19 déc. 1932, 229-30.
.98 RD dated [1932], 231-33.
.99 RD dated [1932], 233-35.
.100 RD dated [1932], 235-36.
.101 RD dated [1932], 236-37.
.102 RD dated [1932], 237-38.
.103 RD dated 22 jan. 1933, 239-41.
.104 Puyaubert, Jean, dated [1933], 243-44.
.105 Puyaubert, Jean, dated 9 mars 1937, 244-45.
.106 Minet, Pierre, dated 4 nov. 1937, 246-47.
.107 Minet, Pierre, dated 22 nov. 1943, 247-48. Repr. Ab366.

Ac281   Aa234 in Jean-Michel Agasse, 'Poétique/Daumal' (Thèse de
         3e cycle, Paris-Nanterre, juin 1971), vol.2, 2-5.

Ab282   'RGL écrit à Renéville [21 juill. 1928]', *La Quinzaine
         Littéraire*, 127 (16 oct. 1971), 14. Repr. Ab366.

Aa283   *Arthur Rimbaud. Frontispiece de Sima. Préface de Bernard
         Noël* (see Bb344). Fata Morgana [Montpellier], coll. 'Scholies',
         no.1, 31 déc. 1971, 61pp., 1205 copies.
         Contains Ab21 and Ab22.1.

1972

RENE DAUMAL

At284   *La Conoscenza di Sè. Scritti et lettere 1939-1941. Opere di RD a
         cura di Claudio Rugafiori, VII.* Translated into Italian by Bianca
         Candian. Adelphi [Milano], febbraio 1972, xiv & 232pp.
         Contains an introduction by Claudio Rugafiori (see Bb351). The
         introduction contains a translation of Ab278.2. The body of the
         text has translations of Ab125, Ab126, As128, Ab129, Ab130,

Ab135, As136, Aa180.1, Ab187.14, Ab187.15, fragments of
Ab198.2, As266.2 (contains FMS) and translations of letters to

.1 Ribemont-Dessaignes, Georges, dated 23 maggio 1939
(extracts), 145-49.

.2 Dermenghem, Emile, dated 31 maggio [1939], 150-54.

.3 Puyaubert, Jean, dated [giugnio 1939], 155-56.

.4 Milanova, Véra, dated 3 luglio [1939] (extracts), 157-59.
Repr. Ab307.

.5 Paulhan, Germaine and Jean, dated 8 luglio [1939],
160-61. Repr. Ab307.

.6 Dermenghem, Emile, dated 8 luglio [1939], 162-63.

.7 Paulhan, Germaine and Jean, dated 19 luglio [1939],
164-65. Repr. Ab307.

.8 Ribemont-Dessaignes, Georges, dated 27-28 luglio [1939]
(extracts), 166-68. Repr. Ab307.

.9 Paulhan, Germaine and Jean, dated 20 agosto 1939
(extracts), 169-70.

.10 Paulhan, Germaine and Jean, dated 5 settembre [1939]
(extracts), 171-72.

.11 Rolland de Renéville, Cassilda and André, dated 29
novembre [1939] (extracts), 173-75.

.12 Dermenghem, Emile, dated 1 aprile [1940] (extracts),
179-81.

.13 Christoflour, Raymond, dated 2 giugnio 1940 (extracts),
182-84.

.14 Daumal, Jack, dated [settembre 1940] (extract), 185-200.
Followed by 3pp. FMS of the letter (201-03). Repr. Ab307
(without the FMS).

.15 Dermenghem, Emile, dated 17 ottobre [1940], 204-07. Repr.
Ab307. (abr.).

.16 Dermenghem, Emile, dated 29 dicembre [1940] (extracts),
208-09.

.17 Dermenghem, Emile, dated 28 gennaio [1941] (extract),
210-11.

.18 Christoflour, Raymond, dated 1 aprile 1941 (extract),
216-18.

.19 Ribemont-Dessaignes, Georges, dated 4 giugnio [1941]
(extract), 219-20.

.20 Rolland de Renéville, Cassilda and André, dated 15 agosto
[1941] (extract), 225.

Ae285   New edition of Ae190, 10 fév. 1972, 478pp.

Ae286   New edition of Ae206, 10 mars 1972, 384pp.

Aa287   *Les Pouvoirs de la Parole. Essais et Notes, II (1935-1943).*

Edition établie par Claudio Rugafiori. Gallimard, nrf,
24 mars 1972, 285pp.
With an introduction and bibliography by Claudio Rugafiori (see
Bb352). Volume repr. Aa343. Contains Ab68, Ab78, Ab83,
Ab84.2, Ab90, Ab91.1, Ab96.1, Ab96.3, Ab97, Ab98, Ab105,
Ab107, Ab110, Ab111.1, Ab111.2, Ab112, Ab115, Ab118,
Ab119.1, Ab119.2, Ab120, Ab121, Ab122, Ab124, Ab129, Ab130,
Ab132, Ab133 (under title 'La Pataphysique et la révélation
du rire (deuxième version)'; also contains the variant version
published in Aa184, here under title 'La Pataphysique et la
révélation du rire (première version)'), Ab135, Ab139, Ac150,
Ab152, Ab163, Ab169 (under title 'Le Père Mot'), Ab181
(under title 'A propos des *Fleurs de Tarbes*'), Aa184.5,
Aa184.7, Aa186, Ab187.1, Ab189, and
   .1 'Lettre à soi-même en forme de parabole', 125-28.
   .2 'Suggestions pour un métier poétique', 153-58.
   .3 '*Le Dict de Padma* (première version)', 169-71.

Aa288   *L'Evidence Absurde. Essais et Notes, I (1926-34). Edition établie
par Claudio Rugafiori*. Gallimard, nrf, 27 mars 1972, 288pp. With
an introduction and a bibliography (see Bb353).
Volume repr. Aa342. Contains Ac4 (under title 'Présentation du
GJ'), Ab6.1, Ab6.3, Ab6.4, Ab9, Ab13, Ab14.1, Ab14.7, Ab14.8,
Ac15.1, Ab16, Ab17, Ab18, Ab33.1, Ab33.3, Ab33.4, Ab35,
Ab48, Ab49, Ab66, Ab67.1, Ab74, Ab76, Aa99.1, Ab183,
Aa184.3, Ab202, Ab254.3 (under title 'L'Asphyxie et l'Evidence
Absurde'), Ab254.4 (under title 'Pseudo-matérialisme et
Emile Meyerson contre la dialectique Hégélienne'), Ab254.5,
Ab254.6, and
   .1 'La Révolte et l'ironie', 101-42. Ch.4 (136-42) previously
      published as Aa184.2. See also Aa271.1.
   .2 'Lettre de Paris', 263-69. Short extract repr. Ab341.

Ae289   New edition of Ae108, Gallimard, coll. 'Folio', no.251,
2 nov. 1972, 512pp.

Aa290   Re-edition of Aa252, 1972.

ROGER GILBERT-LECOMTE

Ab291   Texts in collaboration with RD in Aa288.
Contains Ac10, Ac23.1.

Aa292   *Tétanos mystique*. Same as Ab210. Fata Morgana [Montpellier],
Edition hors-commerce, 31 déc. 1972, 14pp., 19 copies.

1973

RENE DAUMAL

Aa293   *Chansons des marins qui sont à sec de tord-boyaux suivie d'un petit cantique à la Madone Coprolalique.* Fata Morgana [Montpellier], *Edition hors-commerce*, 31 déc. 1973, 16pp. (unpag.), 19 copies.

Ab294   Re-edition of Ab240, 1973.

At295   Poems in bilingual edition under title 'La pelle del mondo, dieci poesie', translated by Bianca Candian, with an introduction by Sergio Solmi (see Bb377), in *Almanacco dello Specchio* [Milano], 2 (1973), 78-101.
Contains Ab29.6, Ab29.8, Ab42.1 (these three previously translated in At239), Ab30.1, Ab55, Aa99.9, Ab187.4, Aa193.15, Aa193.19, Aa193.30.

ROGER GILBERT-LECOMTE

Aa296   *L'Horrible Révélation, la seule... Suivie de notes et fragments inédits. Illustrations de Patrice Vermeille.* Same as Ab39.2.
Fata Morgana [Montpellier], 13 fév. 1973, 78pp, 1000 copies.
Contains Ab166.2, Ab168.2, Ab168.3, Ab168.4, Ab168.5, Aa205.18, Aa205.19, Aa205.21, Aa205.24 and
  .1 Draft plans for 'Retour à Tout', 65-70. Repr. Aa301.
  .2 Four sub-titles for 'Retour à tout', 71.
In the notes there are two poems:
  .3 'Lorsque je m'envole...', 78.
  .4 'Le sansonnet santait [*sic*]...', 78.

1974

RENE DAUMAL

Ac297   Texts in Roger Gilbert-Lecomte, *Œuvres complètes, I. Prose* (Gallimard, nrf, 14 oct. 1974, 371pp.).
Contains Ac5, Ac15.1, Ac15.3, Ac31 and
  .1 'Religion', 105-06. In collaboration with RGL.

Ab298   Texts in Věra Linhartová, *Joseph Sima, ses amis, ses contemporains* (La Connaissance [Bruxelles], coll. 'Témoins et témoignages.

Monographies', 1974, 150pp.).
Contains Ab43 and
   .1 'La Destinée', 124. (FMS)

*At299   Ab141 in *Maitreya* [Berkeley: California], 4 (1974). Translated by Louise Landes Levi.

At300   New edition of At218. Penguin Books Inc. [Baltimore: U.S.A.], 1974, 120pp. With an additional foreword by Jacob Needham (see Bb386).

ROGER GILBERT-LECOMTE

Aa301   *Œuvres complètes, I. Prose. Textes établis et présentés par Marc Thivolet* (see Bb378.2). *Avant-propos de Pierre Minet* (see Bb378.1). Gallimard, nrf, 14 oct. 1974, 371pp. With a bibliography.
In two parts; part 1 under title *Révélation-Révolution* (29-164) contains Ab11, Ab12.1, Ab12.2, Ab12.3, Ab21, Ab22.1, Ac23.1, Ac23.3, Ab24, Ab25, Ab26, Ab36 (includes draft version pp.334-46), Ab37, Ab39.1, Ab39.2, Ab39.3, Ab39.4, Ab41, Ab46, Ab59, Ab257 (under title 'Sima, la peinture et le GJ'), Ab275.5 (with three extra paragraphs), Ab275.6, Ab275.7 (under title 'La Psychanalyse et le GJ') and
   .1 'Psychanalyse. Freud et l'inconscient', 98-101.
   .2 'Le Tabou sexuel', 102-04.
   .3 'Religion', 105-06. In collaboration with RD.
   .4 'Le Fait religieux à travers l'histoire de l'humanité', 107-09.
Part 2 under title *Retour à tout* (165-330) has six sections preceded by a short preface (previously published as Aa205.31).
[Section 1:] *Terreur sur terre ou la vision par l'épiphyse* (167-192) contains Ab123, Ab166.1, Ab166.2, Ab168.1, Ab168.2, Ab168.3, Ab168.4, Ab168.5, Ab171.2, Ab171.3, Ab171.4, Ab171.5, Ab171.6, Ab171.7, Aa205.6, Aa205.7, Aa205.8, Aa205.12, Aa205.13, Aa205.14, Aa205.15, Aa205.16, Aa205.17, Aa205.18, Aa205.19, Aa205.20, Aa205.21, Aa205.22, Aa205.23, Aa205.24, Ab263.9 (without title), Ab263.10, Ab263.11, and
   .5 'Retrouver les souvenirs...', 170.
   .6 'L'impuissance des rêves...', 170.
(the two preceding entries under the title 'Notes diverses')
   .7 'Méditations', 178-80.
   .8 'L'Extase', 181-82.
   .9 'La Vision par l'épiphyse', 182.
   .10 'Après sa mort...', 183-84.

.11 'Problème et parabole', 184-85.

.12 'L'Union par le rêve universel', 185.

.13 'Le Sens de l'être', 185-86.

[Section 2:] *Psychologie des états. Métaphysique expérimentale* (193-205) contains Ab171.8, Ab171.9, Ab171.10, Ab171.11, Aa205.36, and more complete versions of Aa205.40, Aa205.41 and

.14 'La Cathartique du néant. La sublimation de l'Antéros', 198-200.

.15 'Psychologie', 200-03. First section previously published as Aa205.36.

.16 'Notes sur les rapports de l'esthétique et de la paramnésie', 203.

.17 'Sciences', 204-05. Last three notes previously published as Ab171.8, Ab171.9, Ab171.10.

[Section 3:] *Eternité ton nom est non* (207-18) contains

.18 'Le Devenir de l'esprit humain', 209-17.

.19 'Synthèse du devenir', 217-18.

[Section 4:] *Retour à tout* (219-53) contains Ab162.2 (under title 'Acte de dépossession (Tension)'), Ab162.3 (under title 'Raison-système-choc du chaos'), Ab162.4, Ab162.5, Ab162.6, Ab162.7, Aa205.28 (more complete version), Aa205.29 (more complete version), Aa205.30, Aa205.32 (under title 'Fin de l'ère chrétienne. Naissance du troisième homme'), Aa205.33, Aa205.34, Aa205.35, Aa205.37 (without title), Aa205.38, Aa205.39 (without title), and

.20 'Le Problème de l'expression', 223.

.21 'Le Sens de la création', 225.

.22 'Le Problème de l'expression totale dans la durée', 225-26.

.23 'Langage esthétique', 226-28. Last two notes on 227 previously published as Aa205.35.

.24 'Notes diverses', 233-35.

.25 'Mort d'abstraire', 237-40.

.26 'La Dialectique force de l'esprit', 240-41.

.27 'Synthèse dialectique, réduction des antinomies', 241.

.28 'Le Vide plein', 242-43.

.29 'L'Œuvre en acte', 243-44.

.30 'Fondements du pouvoir social', 244-49. Incorporates Aa205.39.

.31 'Créateurs et producteurs', 249-50.

.32 'Magies', 250-53.

[Section 5:] *Notes diverses. Fragments* (255-74) contains

.33 'Valeur de l'art', 257-60.

.34 'Note', 260-61.

.35 'L'Utopie sociale du Marquis de Sade', 261-63.

.36 'Sade, moment ascétique', 264-65.
.37 'Philosophie du sadisme', 265-66.
.38 'Notes critiques', 266-71. Incorporates Aa205.25, Aa205.26.
.39 'Fragment (21e page d'un tout)', 271-73.
.40 'Le Pacifisme', 273.
.41 'Notes', 273-74.
[Section 6:] *Annexe* (275-330) contains three lectures, the
third previously published as Ab275.8:
.42 'Les Métamorphoses de la poésie', 277-94. Delivered
8 Dec. 1932 at the Sorbonne.
.43 'Les Chapelles littéraires modernes [I]', 295-315. Delivered
18 Nov. 1929.
The 'Notes' contain Aa296.1 and
.44 'Préambule annonçant que le seul ennemi du GJ a nom
Sommeil de l'Esprit', 338-39.

1975

RENE DAUMAL

Ab302   Texts in *Argile*, 6 (print. 1975), 140-57. Letters to André
Rolland de Renéville, containing translations from the Sanskrit
(see As303), edited by Jean Richer.
Contains letters to André Rolland de Renéville:
.1   Dated [1933?] (extract), under title ['Les Deux Vérités,
selon Çantiveda]', 140-43. Contains As303.1.
.2   Dated [mars 1933?], under title '[*A-quoi-bons*, traduits du
sanscrit]', 143. Introduction to 'Traductions du sanscrit'
in As303.
.3   Dated [1935] (extract), under title '[Sur l'art poétique
hindou]', 146-50.

As303   Translations, ibid.
.1   'Çantiveda, *La Marche à la lumière (Bodhicaryâvatâra)*,
IX 2-7, IX 56-57, IX 155-58', 140-42.
.2   'Quelques passages de la *Chândogya-Upanishad*', 151-54.
Contains III, 14; IV, 3, iii; V, 3-9.
Under the title 'Traductions du sanscrit' there are 11 short
fragments (144-45), four of which are identified:
.3   '*Lois de Manou (Mânavadharmaçastra)*, II, 135', 144.
.4   'Vichnouçarman, *Pantcha Tantra*, I, 17bis', 144. (Another
version of part of As266.2).
.5   'Çantiveda, *Bodhicaryâvatâra*, VII, 14', 145.
.6   'Bhartrihari, *Nitiçataka*', 145.
.7   Unidentified fragments, 144-45.

ROGER GILBERT-LECOMTE

Ab304   'Lettre [to André Rolland de Renéville, undated]', *Exit*,
5 (print. 1975), 32.

At305   Ab21 and Ab22.1 in *La "superletteratura" e A. Rimbaud*
(Luciano Lucarini [Roma], 11 luglio 1975, xv & 76pp.),
53-71.
Introduced by G[abriele]-A[ldo] Bertozzi (see Bb399).

1976

ROGER GILBERT-LECOMTE

Aa306   *Sophocle: Antigone. Fragment traduit par RGL, avec des
vers de ****. Cymbalum Pataphysicum [Vrigny], coll. 'Les
Astéronymes', no.2, 103 E.P.[1976], 16pp., 999 copies
(*hors-commerce*).
Contains translation of *Antigone*, lines 450-70, accompanied by
FMS. Also contains poems scribbled on FMS and attributed
to RGL:
    .1 'Funambule électrothérapique [attr.]', 10.
    .2 'Ode alphabétique à la beauté décadente [attr.]', 11.
    .3 'Le roi-mage étendait sa puissance fertile...[attr.]', 12.
    .4 'Il sanglotait le pauvre...[attr.]', 12.

1977

RENE DAUMAL

Ab307   Letters under title 'Lettres de la montagne' in *Argile*, 13-14
(print.-été 1977), 184-216. Edited by Claudio Rugafiori.
Contains original versions of At284.4, At284.5, At284.7, At284.8,
At284.14 (without FMS), At284.15 (abr.), and letters to
    .1 Milanova, Véra, dated 10 août [1937] (extracts), 184-85.
    .2 Milanova, Véra, dated 19 août [1937] (extracts), 186-87.
    .3 Milanova, Véra, dated [21 août 1937] (extracts), 187-88.
    .4 Paulhan, Germaine and Jean, dated 10 sept. [1938], 189-90.
    .5 Rolland de Renéville, Cassilda and André, dated 14
       sept. 1938 (extracts), 190-92.
    .6 Ribemont-Dessaignes, Georges, dated 17-21 nov. [1941]
       (extracts), 213-16.

Ab308   *Le Grand Jeu. Collection complète.* Editions Jean-Michel Place, coll. 'Réimpressions des revues d'avant-garde', no.12, 23 août 1977. Facsimile of the three issues of *Le Grand Jeu*, with a partial reconstruction of the fourth. With an introduction by Claudio Rugafiori (see Bb422) and five indexes. Contains Ac5, Ab6.1, Ab6.2, Ab6.3, Ab6.4, Ab14.1, Ab14.2, Ab14.3, Ab14.4, Ab14.5, Ab14.6, Ab14.7, Ab14.8, Ac15.1, Ac15.2, Ac15.3, Ac31 (without title), Ab33.1, Ab33.2, Ab33.3, Ab33.4, Ab33.5, Ac34.1, Aa184.3, complete version of Ab254.2 (as found in Ab269 but without first line), Ab254.3 (without title), Ab254.4 (under title 'Pseudo-matérialisme et Emile Meyerson contre la dialectique hégélienne'), Ab269.1 (under title 'Les Phénoménologistes et le GJ'), Ab269.2.

At309   Translation of Ac5 in At318, 38.

Aa310   New edition of Aa116. *Edition revue et corrigée. Nouvelle édition établie par Claudio Rugafiori.* Gallimard, nrf, 14 nov. 1977, 179pp. Repr. Aa368.

Ac311   Texts written in collaboration with RGL, in Aa319. Contains Aa233 and
.1   'L'Orgie dans le catafalque', 92-93.
.2   'L'Epopée du morpion', 94-95.
.3   'Or un éléphant nain...', 95-96.

As312   'Le Marteau à stupidité (Mohamadgara)', *Port-des-Singes* [L'Hay-les-Roses], 4 (1977), 3pp. (unpag.) [3-5]. With the sub-title 'ébauche de traduction par RD'; followed by FMS of RD's transcription of the original.

Ab313   Letter to Masui, Jacques, dated 30 déc. 1943 (postcard), ibid., one page (unpag.) [6]. (FMS)

Ab314   'Apologue', *Port-des-Singes* [L'Hay-les-Roses], 5 (1977), one page (unpag.), [69].

ROGER GILBERT-LECOMTE

Aa315   *Caves en plein ciel.* Fata Morgana [Montpellier], 1 jan. 1977, 25pp., 333 copies. Accompanied by a separately bound introduction by Claudio Rugafiori (see Bb416), which contains the complete version of Ab263.8.

The volume contains Aa205.10 and
.1 'Agir', 11. Repr. Aa319.
.2 'La Nuit et la fièvre', 12-13. Repr. Aa319.
.3 'Le Taureau noir', 14. Repr. Aa319, Ab339.
.4 'Angoisses', 15-16.
.5 'Eclair prénatal', 17. Repr. Aa319.
.6 'Névrose d'angoisse', 18-20. Repr. Aa319.
.7 'BoXe Match [*sic*]', 21. Repr. Aa319.
.8 'Nuit de bal', 22-24. Repr. Aa319.
.9 'Au sortir du cellier...', 25. Repr. Aa319 [259].

Aa316   *Neuf haï-kaï.* Fata Morgana [Montpellier], 13 fév. 1977, 14pp. (unpag.), 90 copies. Same as Ab2.

Ab317   *Le Grand Jeu. Collection complète.* Editions Jean-Michel Place, coll. 'Réimpressions des revues d'avant-garde', no.12, 23 août 1977. Facsimile of the three issues of *Le Grand Jeu*, with a partial reconstruction of the fourth. With an introduction by Claudio Rugafiori (see Bb422) and five indexes.
Contains Ab11, Ab12.1, Ab12.2, Ab12.3, Ab22.1, Ab22.2, Ab22.3, Ac23.1, Ac23.2, Ac23.3, Ab37 (without title), Ab39.1, Ab39.2, Ab39.3, Ab39.4, Ab39.5, Ac40, Ab275.5 (abr.), Ab275.6, Ab275.7 (under title 'La Psychanalyse et le GJ').

At318   Texts translated into Spanish in *Zona Franca* [Caracas: Venezuela], III, 3 (sept.-oct. 1977), 35-39. Introduced by O.A. (see Bb423.1). Translations by J.E.M.
Under title 'Poemas' contains Aa61.2, Aa61.12, Aa61.32, Aa104.4. Under title 'Sueños' contains Ab196.3, Aa205.4. Under title 'El Gran Juego' contains Ab11. Under title 'Fragmentos' contains Ab171.2, Aa205.9.

Aa319   *Œuvres complètes, II. Poésie. Edition établie par Jean Bolléry. Avant-propos de Pierre Minet* (see Bb429.2). Gallimard, nrf, 14 nov. 1977, xii & 267pp. With preface (see Bb429.1) and bibliography by Jean Bolléry.
In two parts; part one (3-79) contains Aa61, Aa104; part two has three sections:
[Section:] I (81-122) contains Aa211, Aa234, Aa315.7, and
.1 'O! Luna', 85-86.
.2 'Le Pôle sud', 86.
.3 'Révolte', 87.
.4 'Un filou', 88.
.5 'Schampoing [*sic*]', 88.

.6 'Sonnet à B... pour le féliciter de sa nouvelle décoration', 88-89.
.7 'L'Enfantement du Stryge', 89-91.
.8 'Abritez l'abruti...', 104.
.9 'Poème de la saint Charlemagne', 105-10.
.10 'Note: à suivre...', 111.
.11 'Litanie. L'Arme des flagellants', 112-14.
.12 '2e édition de: La Geste du prototype Raoul', 114.
.13 'Un soir de poissons rouges...', 115.
.14 'Esculape trouve une escalope...', 115-16.
.15 'Epithalame', 116-17.
.16 'Voulez-vous, bon marchand...', 117-18.
.17 'Confidence de jeune fille', 118.
.18 'Ce vieillard ridicule...', 118.
.19 'Celle qui fut Héloïse...', 119.
.20 'L'Absence de l'Amour', 119-20.
.21 'Pour les fatales...', 120.
.22 'Il est infiniment...', 121.
.23 'L'Atout du noir', 122.

[Section:] II (123-205) contains two sub-sections; the first, entitled 'Poèmes' (125-183) contains Ab1, Ab2 (details below), Ab159.1, Ab159.2, Ab162.1, Ab171.1, Aa205.1, Aa205.2, Aa205.3, Aa205.9, Aa205.10 (under title 'Tablettes d'un visionné'), Ab210, Ab263.4, Ab263.5, Ab263.6, Ab263.7, Ab263.8 (abr.), Aa280.81, Aa280.82, Aa315.1, Aa315.3, Aa315.5, Aa315.6 (under title 'Angoisse'). Under the title 'Haikais' there are 9 haikus (127-28), 3 previously published as Ab2.4, Ab2.6, Ab2.9; previously unpublished haikus:

.24 'L'aube – Chante l'alouette...', 127.
.25 'Le soleil en feu...', 127.
.26 'Oh! la pleine lune...', 127.
.27 'Les yeux du Chat...', 127.
.28 'J'ai vu en songe...', 128.
.29 'Morte la Déesse...', 128.

(This ends the first group of texts under the title 'Haikais').

.30 'Bouquet sur ma tombe', 128-29.
.31 'Complainte du Yoghi', 129.
.32 'Illusion', 130.

Under the title 'Haikais' there are 26 haikus (132-33), 6 previously published as Ab2.1, Ab2.2, Ab2.3, Ab2.5, Ab2.7, Ab2.8; previously unpublished haikus:

.33 'Sur l'Avril de vert feuillu...', 132.
.34 'Le gros nuage...', 132.

.79 'La Voie', 177.

.80 'De l'auto les deux yeux...', 178.

The second sub-section of [section:] II (185-205) is entitled 'Rêves' and contains Ab22.2, Ab22.3, Ab177, Ab196.1, Ab196.2, Ab196.3, Aa205.4, Aa205.5, Aa205.11, Aa315.2, Aa315.8, and

.81 'Je marche...', 187.

.82 'Eclair de suie', 187-88.

.83 'Quand on sombre sous l'horizon...', 189.

.84 'Autobus...', 192.

.85 'Dancing', 193.

.86 'Cave en plein ciel', 193-94.

.87 'Les Charitiots [*sic*]', 195.

.88 'Venin', 196.

.89 'Convalescence enfantine', 196.

.90 'Rencontre du Mort', 203-04.

.91 'Rêve', 204-05.

[Section:] III (207-20) contains

.92 'Tic Lapeur', 209-20. Fragments of a 'roman poétique'.

In the 'Notes' there are Aa315.9 [259], many variants of previously published items and the following new items:

.93 'Catastrophes...', 225.

.94 Letter to Sima, Joseph, undated (FMS), 226-27.

.95 Letter to Sima, Joseph, dated 5 oct. 1933, 228-29.

.96 'Devenu si petit...', 233.

.97 'A perpétuité', 234.

.98 'Créer', 236.

.99 'Complainte de tout souvenir. Pourquoi, pourquoi et à quoi bon', 242.

.100 'Une dalle béa dans le sol...', 253.

.101 'Révélation originelle...', 254.

.102 'J'ai jeté dans la mer...', 254.

Ac320   Texts in collaboration with RD, ibid.

.1 'L'Orgie dans le catafalque', 92-93.

.2 'L'Epopée du morpion', 94-95.

.3 'Or un éléphant nain...', 95-96.

Ab321   Ab159.1 in *Rouge*, 505 (21 nov. 1977), 10.

1978

RENE DAUMAL

Aa322   *Mugle. Avant-propos de Claudio Rugafiori* (see Bb462). Fata Morgana [Montpellier], 6 oct. 1978, 74pp., 750 copies. Repr. At361.

Ab323   'A une ancienne (ah 'la la [*sic*]) compagne', *Port-des-Singes*
        [L'Hay-les-Roses], 6 (hiv. 1978-1979), 3pp. (unpag.) [53-55].

Ab324   Texts in *L'Originel*, 7, no. sp. 'Le GJ' (déc.-jan.
        [1978-1979]).
        Contains Ac4 (under title 'La Circulaire du *GJ*'), Ac5, Ab6.1,
        Ac15.1, Ab269.2 and
        .1   'Une lettre de RD à Maurice Henry [dated juill. 1926]', 10.

*At325 Ab96.3 in *Text* [New York], 7 (1978). Translated by Louise
        Landes Levi.

ROGER GILBERT-LECOMTE

Ab326   Ab263.8 in *Canal*, 12 (jan. 1978), 5.

Ab327   Ab230 in *Non-lieu*, 2-3, no. sp. 'Benjamin Fondane' (2e trim.
        1978), 30-35.

Ab328   Previously published texts in *L'Originel*, 7, no. sp. 'Le GJ'
        (déc.-jan. [1978-1979]).
        Contains Ac10 (under title 'La Circulaire du *GJ*'), Ab11, Ab22.2,
        Ac23.1, Ab159.2, Ab171.1 (FMS), Ab275.5 (abr.).

Aa329   *Sacra Nox!* Cymbalum Pataphysicum [Courtaumont-par-
        Sermiers], coll. 'Maramoutéenne', no.2, 106 E.P. [1978], 12pp.
        (unpag.), 999 copies. Facsimile of a poem which first appeared
        in a school magazine *Apollo*, 1 (mai 1922). With an anon.
        introduction (see Bb468).

1979

RENE DAUMAL

Ab330   Letter to Sima, Joseph, dated 23 fév. [1933] (extract), in exhibition
        catalogue *Joseph Sima, 1891-1971. Œuvre graphique et amitiés
        littéraires* (Bibliothèque Nationale, 22 mai 1979), 48.

Aa331   *La Soie.* Fata Morgana [Montpellier], 31 déc. 1979, 14 pp.
        (unpag.), 49 copies. With indication 'Ecrit en 1925'. Repr. Ab345.

At332   *A Night of Serious Drinking.* Aa116 translated by David Coward and E.A. Lovatt. Routledge and Kegan Paul [London], 1979, ix & 150pp. Repr. At333.

At333   Same as At332. Shambhala Publications [Boulder: Colorado], 1979, 121pp. Repr. At364.

ROGER GILBERT-LECOMTE

Ab334   'Notes envoyées à Joseph Sima pour le décor d'une pièce de théâtre', in exhibition catalogue *Joseph Sima, 1891-1971. Œuvre graphique et amitiés littéraires* (Bibliothèque Nationale, 22 mai 1979), 47. Includes FMS of one page.

1980

RENE DAUMAL

Ab335   Previously published texts in catalogue to the exhibition *Le GJ* held at the Maison de la Culture du Havre, Jan. 1980, 38pp. (unpag.).
Contains Ac4, Ac5, and
.1   'Le Casse-dogme', item 104 (FMS note), [26].

Aa336   Second edition of Aa310, 19 sept. 1980, 184pp.

Ac337   Ac47 and Ac56 in *Tracts surréalistes et déclarations collectives. Tome I, 1922-1939* (Le Terrain Vague, oct. 1980, 544pp.), 208-22, 238-40.

Ab338   Ab88 in Virmaux, Odette & Virmaux, Alain, *Artaud Vivant* (Nouvelles Editions Oswald, coll. 'Lumière sur', no.1. nov. 1980, 352pp.), 197-203.
Introduced by the authors (see Bb486).

ROGER GILBERT-LECOMTE

Ab339   Previously published texts in catalogue to the exhibition *Le GJ* held at the Maison de la Culture du Havre, Jan. 1980, 38pp. (unpag.).
Contains Ac10, Ab11, draft of Ab24, Ab39.3 (FMS), Aa315.3 and
.1   Plan for 'Ce que devrait être la peinture, ce que sera Sima', item 138 (FMS), [30].

Ac340   Ac53, Ac60 and Ac79 in *Tracts surréalistes et déclarations collectives. Tome I, 1922-1939* (Le Terrain Vague, oct. 1980, 544pp.), 208-22, 238-40, 262-64.

1981

RENE DAUMAL

Ab341   Short extract from Aa288.2 in Virmaux, Alain & Virmaux, Odette, *RGL et le GJ* (Belfond, 1er trim. 1981, 283pp.), 215.

Aa342   Second edition of Aa288, 9 jan. 1981, 288pp.

Aa343   Second edition of Aa287, 9 jan. 1981, 286pp.

Aa344   *Le Mont Analogue. Roman d'aventures alpines, non euclidiennes et symboliquement authentiques. Version définitive.* Gallimard, coll. 'L'Imaginaire', no.72, 4 mars 1981, 177pp.
Aa180 edited by H.J[osèphe] Maxwell and C[laudio] Rugafiori. With an introduction (see Bb494) and an appendix which contains the introduction and conclusion of Ab125; Aa180.5 (with three additional previously unpublished paragraphs, 172-74); a plan for ch.5 (158); and FMS plan of chs.5-7 (159).

Ab345   'Textes' in *RD ou le retour à soi (Textes inédits et études)* (L'Originel, 11 sept. 1981, 304pp.), 17-96.
In six sections:
[Section 1:] *Ecrits de jeunesse (1925-1926)* contains Aa331 and
    .1 'Le Naufrage du linge', 22.
    .2 'Rêve', 23.
    .3 'L'ombre a toujours pris...', 24.
    .4 'Un garçon naquit...', 25.
    .5 'La maison du sommeil...', 26-27.
[Section 2:] *Poétique (1931-1938)* contains
    .6 'Questionnaire', 31-32.
    .7 'La Transmission de la pensée', 33-34.
    .8 'L'Art hindou', 35-37. Draft version of Ab109.
[Section 3:] *Hymne au Soma* contains FMS of Aa265.2; under title 'La Vision-des-stances, IX cycle (L'Offrande de la liqueur)' As266.1 (with FMS) as '1ère version', As241 as '2e version'; previously unpublished translations (see As346).
[Section 4:] *Un maître de liberté: D.T. Suzuki* contains Ae138, Ae143.
[Section 5:] *Bhartrhari III,15, III,87* contains two fragments,

the first previously published as As136.6, the second as
As266.4. Both accompanied by the FMS of the Sanskrit text,
transcription and translation.
[Section 6:] *Textes de 1942* contains Ab140, Ab142 and
  .9 Letter to Lief, Geneviève, dated 19 août 1942, 93-95.
Scattered through the volume are various FMS: Ac15.1
(previously published as part of Ab335), and
  .10 'Ordre de la révolte', 96. With the indication 'Note pour
     le premier numéro du *GJ*'.
  .11 'C'est le propre de la pensée métaphysique...', 168. With
     the indication 'Manuscrit, vers 1928-1929'.
  .12 'Intuition métaphysique dans l'histoire', 204. With the
     indication 'Manuscrit, 1932'.
Also contains errata for Aa271 on p.299.

As346   Translations in Ab345:
  .1 'La Vision-des-stances, IXe cycle, 15.727 (L'Offrande de
     la liqueur) (2e version) [*Rig-Veda*]', 45.
  .2 'Hymne XVIII [*Rig-Veda*] 18.730', 46.
  .3 'Hymne XXVI [*Rig-Veda*] 26.738', 47.
  .4 'Hymne XLII [*Rig-Veda*] 42.753', 48.

At347   'Le Grand Jeu. Einführung, Textauswahl und Übersetzung, von
Gerd Henniger', previously published texts translated into German
in *Akzente* [München], XXVIII, 6 (Dez. 1981), 499-534.
Contains an introduction (see Bb515) and translations of Ac5,
Ab6.1, Ab254.3.

Ab348   Ab152 in 'Lettres à Léon-Gabriel Gros', *Sud* [Marseille],
41-42 (déc. 1981), 108-10.

At349   *Das Große Besäufnis*. Aa116 translated into German by Brigitte
Weidmann, Henssel/CVK Bielef [Berlin], 1981, 184pp.

ROGER GILBERT-LECOMTE

Ab350   Same as Aa237.1 in Virmaux, Alain & Virmaux, Odette,
RGL et le GJ (Belfond, 1er trim. 1981, 283pp.), 237.

Ab351   Letter to Caillois, Roger, dated 30 jan. 1930, *Roger Caillois.
Cahiers pour un temps* (Centre Georges Pompidou/Pandora
Editions, 31 août 1981, 260pp.), 180-81.

At352   'Le Grand Jeu. Einführung, Textauswahl und Übersetzung, von

Gerd Henniger', previously published texts translated into German in *Akzente* [München], XXVIII, 6 (Dez. 1981), 499-534. Contains an introduction (see Bb515) and translations of Ab11, Ab12.1, Ab39.2.

1982

RENE DAUMAL

*At353 *Der Analog.* New edition of At229. Suhrkamp/KNO [Frankfurt-am-Main], 'Bibliothek Suhrkamp', no.802, 1982, 190pp.

At354 *La Montaña Análoga. Novela de aventuras alpinas no euclidianas y simbólicamente autenticas.* Translation of Aa344 by Carmen Santos. Alfaguara [Madrid], junio 1982, 159pp. Repr. At361a.

At355 *Rasa, or, Knowledge of the Self. Essays on Indian Aesthetics and Selected Sanskrit Studies.* Translated with an introduction (see Bb531) by Louise Landes Levi. New Directions [New York], 1982, 112pp.
Contains Ab48, Ab49, As92, As128, Ab129, As136 (without final 'notice'), As227, As243.3 (together with the second version from Aa265), Aa265.2 (abr.). Section entitled 'Oriental Book Reviews' contains Ab68, Ab96.1, Ab111.2, Ab112, Ab121. Many of the bibliographical details given in this volume, such as dates of first publication, are wrong.

ROGER GILBERT-LECOMTE

Aa356 *Poèmes et chroniques retrouvés. Présentés par Alain et Odette Virmaux* (see Bb524.1, Bb524.2). Rougerie [Mortemart], 15 mars 1982, 78pp., 2250 copies.
Contains Ab114, Ab134, Ac146, Ac147, Ac148, Ac149, Ab162.1 (FMS), and
.1 'Anti-soleil', 17. FMS on 10.
.2 'Vieux précepte du monde mort', 18. FMS on 10.
.3 'Clin d'œil', 19. FMS on 10.

*Ab357 Two letters in *Cahiers de Mauregny*, 11 (1982).
.1 Letter to Rolland de Renéville, André, dated [1928].
.2 Letter to Rolland de Renéville, André, dated 16 mars 1928.

1983

RENE DAUMAL

Ab358   'Salut citoyens!', FMS of satirical advertisement for joining the army under title 'Dos páginas escritas por RD en 1929' in José-Carlos Cataña, 'El absoluto, o si no cualquier cosa. RD hermano simplista', *Quimera*, 28 (febr. 1983), 16-21 (FMS on 20).

1984

RENE DAUMAL

Ab359   Ac15.2 and Ab18 in *Rimbaldiana* [Charleville-Mézières], no.sp. 'Rimbaud. RD, Roger Vailland, RGL' (2e trim. 1984).

Ab360   Same as Aa184.1 in catalogue of the 'Exposition RD' held at the Lycée Chanzy 16-21 Apr. 1984 and the Musée Rimbaud 25 Apr.-20 May 1984, both in Charleville-Mézières. Edited by Pascal Sigoda and Annie Bissarette (2e trim. 1984 [Charleville-Mézières], 42pp.), 37-40.

*At361 Same as Aa322 translated into Italian by G.P. Baiocchi, a cura di Claudio Rugafiori. Cavaliere Azzurro [Bologna], 1984, 72pp.

At361a Reprint of At354, sept. 1985.

ROGER GILBERT-LECOMTE

Ab362   Ab22.1 and Ac23.2 in *Rimbaldiana* [Charleville-Mézières], no.sp. 'Rimbaud. RD, Roger Vailland, RGL' (2e trim. 1984).

1985

RENE DAUMAL

Ab363   Ac34.1, Ab187.11 in Roland Dumas, *Plaidoyer pour RGL. Avec la collaboration de Christine Piot suivi de Le Cristal dans l'éclair par Serge Sautreau* (Gallimard, nrf, 10 mai 1985, 256pp.).

At364   Re-edition of At333, Sept. 1985.

Aa365   *La Langue sanskrite. Grammaire. Poésie. Théâtre.* No publisher indicated (© 1985, Jack Daumal et Société des amis de RD). FMS of RD's personal Sanskrit grammar [160pp.] (132pp. with 14 intercalated pp. reproduced as 'Annexes'). 310 copies.

ROGER GILBERT-LECOMTE

Ab366   Texts in Roland Dumas, *Plaidoyer pour RGL. Avec la collaboration de Christine Piot suivi de Le Cristal dans l'éclair par Serge Sautreau* (Gallimard, nrf, 10 mai 1985, 256pp.). Contains Ac40, Aa280.19, Aa280.21, Aa280.107, Ab282, many short extracts from Aa280, and
.1   Draft of last will and testament dated 24 avr. 1943, 85.
and the following letters to
.2   Pierre-Quint, Léon, dated 4 sept. 1939, 77-78.
.3   Lecomte, Edmond, dated 12 août 1942 (draft telegram), 84.
.4   Lecomte, Edmond, undated draft, 86-88.
.5   Lecomte, Edmond, undated draft, 88-89.
.6   Laire, Paul, undated draft, 89-91.
.7   Bataille, Georges, dated 13 jan. 1930, 201-02.
.8   Desnos, Robert, dated 2 août 1934 (telegram), 202.
.9   Foujita-Desnos, Youki, dated 17 juin 1935, 203.
.10 Firmat, Mme, undated, 203-04.
.11 Firmat, Mme, dated 17 août 1941 (I.O.U.), 217.

Aa367   *Lettre à Benjamin Fondane. Avant lettre par Serge Sautreau* (see Bb567.1). Same as Ab230. Les Cahiers des Brisants [St-Pierre-du-Mont: Mont-de-Marsan]. Livres de Nulle Part, coll. 'Le GJ', 4 nov. 1985, 30pp. 530 copies.

1986

RENE DAUMAL

Aa368   Same as Aa310 (with the exception of a short bio-bibliography on p.5), Gallimard, coll. 'L'Imaginaire', no.165, 14 fév. 1986, 174pp.

At369   Same as At218 but with title of At219 and translations of additional material as found in Aa344. Penguin Books [Harmondsworth: Middlesex], 'King Penguin' series, 1986, 128pp.

*At370 New edition of At219. Shambhala [Boulder: Colorado], Oct. 1986, 114pp.

1987

RENE DAUMAL

At371 *A Fundamental Experiment.* Hanuman Books [New York], Sept. 1987, 68pp.
Translation of Ab163 by Roger Shattuck; with translator's note (see Bb580).

ROGER GILBERT-LECOMTE

At372 Texts in *Literary Review* [Madison, New Jersey], XXX, 3, no.sp. 'New Writing in French' (Spring 1987), 472-74.
Contains Aa104.3, Ab159.2, Ab171.1, Ab263.8, translated by David Rattray.

SECONDARY MATERIAL

1923

Bb1   Maublanc, René, 'Deux vrais jeunes', *Le Pampre* [Reims], 7-8 ([fév.] 1923), 13.
Introduction to Ab1. Extract repr. Ba488. Full version repr. Bb429, Ba559. [RGL]

1928

Bb2   Robert, Francis, 'Revue des revues', *1928*, 29 ([juill.] 1928), 243. [Le GJ]

Bb3   *Anon.*, 'La Revue des Revues: Jeunes', *Les Nouvelles Littéraires*, 299 (7 juill. 1928), 9. [Le GJ]

Bb4   [Gaillard, André], 'Revue des revues', *CdS*, V, 104 (août-sept. 1928), 152. [CR *Le GJ* I]

Bb5   Godmé, Jean, 'Lettre au Grand Jeu sur la vertu de la pureté', *1928*, 3 ([août] 1928), 109-16.

Bb6   Crouzet, Guy, 'Naissance de *Le GJ*', *La Grande Revue*, 8 (août 1928), 340-42. [Le GJ]

Bb7   Hirsch, Charles-Henry, 'Le GJ', *Mercure de France*, CCVI, 724 (15 août 1928), 184-85. [CR *Le GJ* I]

Bb8   Pierre-Quint, Léon, 'Le GJ ou un signe dans l'avenir', *Les Nouvelles Littéraires*, 312 (6 oct. 1928), 4. Repr. Ba283, Ba559. [CR *Le GJ* I]

1929

Bb9   A[ragon], L[ouis] & B[reton], A[ndré], 'A suivre. Petite

contribution au dossier de certains intellectuels à tendances révolutionnaires (Paris 1929)', *Variétés* [Bruxelles], no.hors série, 'Le Surréalisme en 1929' (juin 1929), i-xxxiii.
Account of the meeting at the Bar du Château, 11 March 1929.
Repr. Bb485; extracts repr. Bb45, Ba283. [Le GJ]

Bb10   Crouzet, Guy, 'Quelques revues d'avant-garde', *La Grande Revue*, 7 (juill. 1929), 157-58. [CR *Le GJ* II]

Bb11   Breton, André, 'Second Manifeste du Surréalisme', *La Révolution Surréaliste*, 12 (15 déc. 1929), 12-13. Repr. Bb14, Bb39, Bb165. [RD]

1930

Bb12   Pierre-Quint, Léon, *Le Comte de Lautréamont et Dieu* (*CdS*, collection critique, no.8, 20 jan. 1930 [copyright 1929], 168pp.). RGL mentioned 7, 13-14. Repr. Bb201, Ba559.

Bb13   Teige, Karel, 'Nadrealismus a Vysoká Hra', *ReD*, [*sic*: abbreviation for *Revue Devĕtsil*] [Praha], no.sp. 'Le GJ', 8 ([Summer] 1930), 249-55.
Translated extract repr. Ba488.

Bb14   Breton, André, same as Bb11 (Kra, 25 juin 1930, 106pp.), 67-68.

1931

Bb15   Gueguen, Pierre, 'Actualités poétiques', *Les Nouvelles Littéraires*, 430 (10 jan. 1931), 7. [CR *Le GJ* III]

Bb16   Gueguen, Pierre, 'Actualités poétiques', *Les Nouvelles Littéraires* 440 (21 mars 1931), 7. [CR Ab42]

Bb17   Bernier, Jean, *La Critique Sociale*, 2 (1931). Repr. Bb467. [CR *Le GJ* III]

1933

Bb18   Pierre-Quint, Léon, 'Prière d'insérer', in Aa61. Repr. Bb429.

1934

Bb19   Cassou, Jean, 'Poésie', *Les Nouvelles Littéraires*, 536 (6 jan. 1934), 2. [CR Aa61]

Bb20   Bertelé, René, *CdS*, XI, 161 (avr.-mai 1934), 308-09. [CR Aa61]

Bb21   Artaud, Antonin, *NRF*, XLIII, 255 (déc. 1934), 925-27. Extract repr. Ba488. Full version repr. Bb160, Bb374, Ba559. [CR Aa61]

1935

Bb22   Rougemont, Denis de, *NRF,* XLV, 264, (sept. 1935), 460-62. [CR Ab83]

1937

Bb23   Rolland de Renéville, A[ndré], *NRF,* XLVIII, 282 (mars 1937), 448-50. Repr. Bb31. [CR Aa99]

1938

Bb24   Gros, Léon-Gabriel, *CdS,* XVII, 209 (oct. 1938), 730. [CR Aa104]

1939

Bb25   Rolland de Renéville, A[ndré], *NRF,* LII, 309 (juin 1939), 1049-52. [CR Aa116]

Bb26   Christoflour, Raymond, 'Le Mouvemont des idées. Antimodernes', *Mercure de France,* CCXCIII, 987 (1 août 1939), 657-59. [CR Aa116]

1940

Bb27   Raymond, Marcel, *De Baudelaire au Surréalisme* (José Corti, 1940, 367pp.), 357-58. Repr. Bb42. [RD]

1941

Bb28   Clancier, G[eorges]-E[mmanuel], 'La Guerre sainte', *Fontaine* [Alger], 13 (mars 1941), 280. [CR Aa127]

1942

Bb29   Larcher, Hubert, *Fusées* [Marseille], 2 (7 juin 1942), 11-13. Repr. Ba512. [CR Ab131]

1944

Bb30   Texts in *CdS*, XXI, 226 (juin-juill. 1944) under title 'In Memoriam RGL'.
    .1   Minet, Pierre, 391-96. Repr. Ba488.
    .2   P[ierre]-Q[uint], Léon, 397-401. Repr. Ba488.

Bb31   Rolland de Renéville, André, 'Deux poètes de la connaissance', in *L'Univers de la parole* (Gallimard, 15 nov. 1944, 212pp.), 159-170 (165-70 same as Bb23).
Extract repr. Ba488. [RGL, RD]

1945

Bb32   Nadeau, Maurice, *Histoire du surréalisme* (Seuil, coll. 'Pierres vives', 2e trim. 1945, 368pp.), 154-56, 172-75.
Repr. Bb133, Bb177, Bb187, Bb246, Bb272. [Le GJ]

Bb33   'Souvenir de RD', *CdS*, XXIII, 272 ([août] 1945), 506-17.
Contains a text by RD (Ab161) and four untitled pieces:
    .1   Rolland de Renéville, A[ndré], 506-09.
    .2   Dermenghem, Emile, 509-10.
    .3   Bousquet, Joë, 511.
    .4   D[aumal], V[éra] M[ilanova], 512-13. Introduction to Ab161.

Bb34   Adamov, Arthur, introduction to Ab162, 33. [RGL]

1946

Bb35   Adamov, Arthur, introduction to Ab166, 23-24. [RGL]

Bb36   Adamov, Arthur, *L'Aveu* (Sagittaire, 2e trim. 1946, 164pp.).
        RGL mentioned on 7 & 80. Repr. Bb260, Ba559.

Bb37   'RD (1908-1944)', *Fontaine* [Alger], IX, 52 (mai 1946).
        Contains two texts by RD (see Ab164) and
        .1   F[ouchet], M[ax]-P[ol], introduction, 779.
        .2   *Anon.*, bio-bibliography, 779.
        .3   Hell, Henri, 'Note sur RD', 780-87.

Bb38   Noulet, E[milie], 'Les Cahiers de la Pléiade', *Constellation,*
        66 (4e trim. 1946), 119-20.
        Repr. Bb181. [CR Ab163]

1947

Bb39   Breton, André, Bb11 in *Les Manifestes du Surréalisme suivis de
        Prologomènes à un troisième Manifeste du Surréalisme ou non*
        (Sagittaire, 1er trim. 1947 [copyright 1946], 216pp.), 162-3. [RD]

Bb40   Minet, Pierre, *La Défaite* (Sagittaire, 25 avr. 1947, 280pp.)
        Many refs to RGL, RD, & Le GJ. Repr. Bb369.

Bb41   Juin, Hubert, 'La Transmutation refusée', *Centre,* 9 (nov. 1947),
        53-59. [RD]

Bb42   Raymond, Marcel, new edition of Bb27, 1947, same pagination.

1948

Bb43   Vailland, Roger, *Le Surréalisme contre la révolution* (Editions
        sociales, 1er trim. 1948, 64pp.).
        Le GJ discussed 25-26, 28-29, 33-34, 37. Repr. Bb555.

Bb44   François, Bernard, 'Le GJ, naissance et place historique',
        Cheval Blanc, 2-3 (mars-avr. 1948), 7-17.
        In no. entitled 'Le Temps de l'amitié', under section
        'Tentatives sans lendemain'.

Bb45   Aragon, Louis & Breton, André, extracts from Bb9 in Nadeau,
        Maurice, *Histoire du surréalisme, II. Documents surréalistes*
        (Seuil, coll. 'Pierres vives', 2e trim. 1948, 400pp.), 132-43.

Bb46   Robert, Marthe & Adamov, Arthur, 'RGL', *Mercure de France,*

CCCIV, 1022 (1 oct. 1948), 257-60.
Introduction to Ab171. Expanded version repr. Bb101.

1952

Bb47 Texts in Aa180.
.1 Rolland de Renéville, A[ndré], 'Préface', 11-23. [RD]
.2 Daumal, Véra, 'Postface', 193-97. Repr. Bb152, Bb155, Bb163, Bb219, Bb225 (abr.), Bb227, Bb363, Bb386, Bb576. [RD]

Bb48 Pauwels, Louis, 'Une société secrète: les disciples de G. Gurdjieff', *Arts,* 357 (1 mai 1952), 5. [RD]

Bb49 Lobet, Marcel, 'La Vie littéraire', *Revue Générale Belge* [Liège] (mai 1952), 167. [CR Aa180]

Bb50 Rousseaux, André, 'L'Ascension du Mont Analogue', *Le Figaro Littéraire,* 316 (10 mai 1952), 2.
Repr. Bb93. [CR Aa180]

Bb51 Breton, André, *Entretiens 1913-1952* (Gallimard, nrf, coll. 'Le Point du jour', 31 juill. 1952, 320pp.), 148.
Repr. Bb271, Bb366. [Le GJ]

Bb52 Grison, Pierre, 'Vers le Mont Analogue', *France-Asie* [Saigon], VIII, 75 (août 1952), 570-75. [CR Aa180]

Bb53 Laffont-Bompiani, 'La Grande Beuverie', *Dictionnaire des Œuvres. II* (S.E.D.E.S., 4e trim. 1952, 680pp.), 466. [CR Aa116].

Bb54 Méautis, Georges, 'Un initié, RD', *Le Lotus Bleu,* 6 (nov.-dec. 1952), 161-71.
Repr. Bb140. [CR Aa180]

1953

Bb55 Sainmont, J.-H., *Les Lettres Nouvelles,* 1 (mars 1953), 106-07. [CR Aa180]

Bb56 Daumal, Véra, 'Note', in Aa184, 7-8. [RD]

Bb57   Petitfaux, Georges, *Les Lettres Nouvelles,* 5 (juill. 1953), 612-14.
        [CR Aa184]

Bb58   Rousseaux, André, 'L'Œuvre en marche de RD', *Le Figaro Littéraire*, 376 (4 juill. 1953), 2.
        Repr. Bb93. [CR Aa184]

Bb59   Marion, Denis, 'Exploration sans retour', *Le Soir* [Bruxelles], 204 (25 juill. 1953), 7. [CR Aa180, Aa184]

Bb60   Nimier, Roger, 'RD: I — A la recherche de la vérité', *Carrefour*, 463 (29 juill. 1953), 9.
        Repr. Bb176, Bb183. [CR Aa184]

Bb61   Kemp, Robert, 'Les Hommes traqués', *Les Nouvelles Littéraires*, 1352 (30 juill. 1953), 2. [CR Aa180]

Bb62   Mars, Paul-Claude, 'La Poésie et l'aventure', *La Dépêche du Midi* [Toulouse], 1766 (31 juill. 1953), 1-2. [CR Aa180]

Bb63   Blanchard, Charles, *Le Petit Crapouillot*, 8 (août 1953), 1 p. (unpag., [3]). [CR Aa184]

Bb64   Nimier, Roger, 'RD: II — Le lyrisme et l'ironie', *Carrefour*, 464 (5 août 1953), 9.
        Repr. Bb176, Bb183.

Bb65   Coiplet, Robert, 'René Guénon, présenté par M. Paul Sérant', *Le Monde,* 2672 (29 août 1953), 7. [CR Aa184]

Bb66   Dort, Bernard, *CdS*, XXXVII, 317 ([sept.] 1953), 159-60.
        [CR Aa180]

Bb67   Perros, Georges, *NRF*, II, 9 (1 sept. 1953), 526-27.
        Repr. Bb507. [CR Aa184]

Bb68   C., J., 'RD ou le besoin d'évasion', *La Libre Belgique* [Bruxelles], 245 (2 sept. 1953), 10. [CR Aa184]

Bb69   Le Clec'h, Guy, *La Table Ronde*, 70 (oct. 1953), 129-30.
        [CR Aa184]

1954

Bb70   Girard, Marcel, *Guide illustré de la littérature française moderne (de 1918 à aujourd'hui)* (Seghers, *nouvelle édition mise à jour*, 1er trim. 1954, 272pp.), 183 (in section 'Recherches sur la poésie'). Repr. Bb164, Bb235. [RD]

Bb71   Pauwels, Louis, *Monsieur Gurdjieff* (Seuil, 1er trim. 1954, 448pp.). Part 4, ch.1 (385-92) & ch.9 (430-37) on RD. Latter contains letters:
.1   Minet, Pierre, Letter to Louis Pauwels, 431-35.
.2   Rolland de Renéville, André, Letter to Louis Pauwels, 435-36.

Bb72   [Paulhan Jean], 'La Guerre sainte', *NRF*, III, 13 (1 jan. 1954), 168-69. [RD]

Ba73   Texts in *CdS*, no. sp. 'Il y a dix ans RD', XXXVIII, 322 (mars 1954). Contains texts by RD (see Ab187) and
.1   Rainord, Manuel, 'RD miroir des hommes', 345-52.
.2   Gros, Léon-Gabriel, 'RD et "Le GJ"', 353-57.
.3   Dort, Bernard, 'Un penseur révolutionnaire', 358-61.
.4   *Anon.*, 'Notice' (bio-bibliography), 362.
.5   Masui, Jacques, 'RD et l'Inde', 381-86.

Bb74   Schwab, Raymond, *Mercure de France*, 1087 (1 mars 1954), 539-43. [CR Aa184]

Bb75   Adamov, Arthur, 'Notes' for Ab196, 461. [RGL]

Bb76   Rousseaux, André, 'Une affaire mystico-religieuse: Gurdjieff et ses disciples', *Le Figaro Littéraire*, 411 (6 mars 1954), 2. Repr. Bb93. [CR Bb71]

Bb77   Rousseaux, André, corrigendum for Bb76, *Les Nouvelles Littéraires*, 414 (27 mars 1954), 2. [RD]

Bb78   Lehner, Frederick, *Books Abroad* [Norman: Oklahoma], XXVIII, 3 (Summer 1954), 321. [CR Aa193]

Bb79   Grison, Pierre, 'Formes et formules traditionnelles.IV.Valeur actuelle du Yoga', *France-Asie* [Saigon], X, 99 (août 1954), 1091-98 (1097). [CR Aa184]

Bb80   C., Jl., *Pour l'Art* [Lausanne], 38 (sept.-oct.1954), 34. [CR Aa184]

Bb81   Daumal, Véra, 'A propos de Gurdjieff et de RD', *NRF*, IV, 22 (1 oct. 1954), 720-21.

Bb82   D[aumal], V[éra], 'Note', introduction to Aa193, 8. [RD]

Bb83   Mauriac, Claude, 'L'Enigmatique [R]D', *Le Figaro*, 3176
(24 nov. 1954), 13. [CR Aa193]

Bb84   Rousselot, Jean, *Les Nouvelles Littéraires*, 1422 (2 déc. 1954), 3.
[CR Aa193]

Bb85   Rousseaux, André, 'La Poésie de RD', *Le Figaro Littéraire*, 451
(11. déc. 1954), 2. [CR Aa193]

Bb86   Texts in *Cahiers du Collège de Pataphysique*, 8-9 (80 E.P.[1954]).
Contains 'Julien Torma: Correspondance avec RD' (anonymously
annotated):
   .1   Torma, Julien, Letter to RD, dated 'Pentecôte 1926', 46.
   .2   Torma, Julien, Letter to RD, dated 6 avr. 1927, 48-49.
   .3   Torma, Julien, Letter to RD, dated 20 oct. 1929, 50-52.
Followed by
   .4   Torma, Julien, 'Lettre à Jean Montmort', dated 2 nov. 1929,
      52-53. [RD]

1955

Bb87   L[oranquin], Alb[ert], *Bulletin des Lettres* [Lyon], 164 (15 jan.
1955), 21-22. [CR Aa193]

Bb88   Magny, Olivier de, *Les Lettres Nouvelles*, 24 (fév. 1955), 281. [CR
Aa193]

Bb89   Daumal Véra, 'Note', introduction to Ab198, 280. [RD]

Bb90   Roy, Claude, 'Le Rendez-vous des poètes' *Libération*, 3243
(9 fév. 1955), 2. [CR Aa193]

Bb91   Thée, Pierre, 'Poésie noire ou blanche?', *La Tribune de Genève*
[Genève], 36 (12 fév. 1955), 7. [CR Aa193]

Bb92   Lecrique, Camille, 'Poésie', *La Grive* [Charleville-Mézières], 85
(mars 1955), 31-32. [CR Aa193]

Bb93   Rousseaux, André, 'L'Avènement de RD', in *Littérature du XXe
siècle*, vol.5 (Albin Michel, mars 1955, 272pp.), 35-57.
Contains Bb50, Bb58, Bb76. [RD]

Bb94   Rode, Henri, *La Table Ronde*, 87 (mars 1955), 154-55. [CR Aa193]

Bb95   Saint-Ideuc, J[ean]-M[arie] de, 'Lettre d'été, *Le Goéland* [Dinard], 116 (avr. 1955), 1p. (unpag.[4]). [CR Aa193]

Bb96   T[anner], A[ndré], *Pour l'Art* [Lausanne], 42 (mai-juin 1955), 32-33. [CR Aa193]

Bb97   Estang, Luc, 'RD(1)', *Revue de la Pensée Française,* XIV, 5 (mai 1955), 57-60.

Bb98   Blanchard, Charles, *Le Petit Crapouillot*, 6 (juin 1955), 1p. (unpag.[3]). [CR Aa193]

Bb99   Estang, Luc, 'RD(2)', *Revue de la Pensée Française*, XIV, 6 (juin 1955), 49-52.

Bb100   Mathias, Pierre, *CdS*, XLI, 330 (août 1955), 333-34. [CR Aa193]

Bb101   Texts in Aa205.
       .1   Adamov, Arthur, 'Introduction' (expanded version of Bb46), 7-15. [RGL]
       .2   Minet, Pierre, 'Avant-propos', 17-18. [RGL]

Bb102   Grison, Pierre, 'Requiem pour un disciple', *France-Asie* [Saigon], XII, 113 (oct. 1955), 267-73. [RD]

Bb103   Michaud, Marcel, 'RD', *Reflets* [Lyon] (nov. 1955), 16. Accompanies Ab201. [RD]

Bb104   Mauriac, Claude, 'RGL', *Le Figaro*, 3469 (2 nov. 1955), 11. [CR Aa205]

Bb105   Rousseaux, André, 'L'Enfant poète et le poète mort', *Le Figaro Littéraire*, 498 (5 nov. 1955), 2. [CR Aa205]

Bb106   Morvan, J.-J., 'Portrait d'un grand écrivain inconnu', *L'Express*, 147 (8 nov. 1955), 8. [CR Aa205]

Bb107   Jaccottet, Philippe, 'Variations sur Büchner, le froid et le feu', *Gazette de Lausanne [Littéraire]* [Lausanne], 268 (12 nov. 1955), 10. [CR Aa205]

Bb108 L[oranquin], Alb[ert], *Bulletin des Lettres* [Lyon], 172 (15 nov. 1955), 365. [CR Aa205]

Bb109 Frontes, Stéphane, 'Le Testament universel de RGL', *Carrefour*, 585 (30 nov. 1955), 9. [CR Aa205]

Bb110 Magny, Olivier de, *Les Lettres Nouvelles*, 33 (déc. 1955), 795-97. [CR Aa205]

Bb111 Oster, Pierre, *NRF*, VI, 36 (1 déc. 1955), 1142-1147. [CR Aa205]

Bb112 Bosquet, Alain, 'L'Instinct et la volonté', *Combat*, 3558 (8 déc. 1955), 7. [CR Aa205]

Bb113 Brenner, Jacques, *Paris-Normandie* [Rouen], 3482 (16 déc. 1955), 9. [CR Aa205]

Bb114 Braun, Benoîte, *Beaux-Arts*, (23 déc. 1955). [CR Aa205]

Bb115 Sartoris, Michel, 'Un poète maudit: RGL', *Demain* (29 déc. 1955). [CR Aa205]

Bb116 Sainmont, J.-H., 'Avertissement', introduction to Ab202. [RD]

1956

Bb117 Grossreider, Hans, 'Dichtung und Innerlichkeit zum Werk RDs', *Schweizer Rundschau* [Zürich], LV, 10 (Jan. 1956), 578-82. [RD]

Bb118 Lecomte, Marcel, 'Destin de RGL', *Le Journal des Poètes* [Dilbeek: Bruxelles], XXVI, 2 (fév. 1956), 2.
Modified version repr. Bb131. [CR Aa205]

Bb119 Kim, Jean-Jacques, *La Table Ronde*, 98 (fév. 1956), 157-58.
Extract repr. Ba488. [CR Aa205]

Bb120 Youngblood, Sarah, *Books Abroad* [Norman: Oklahoma], 2 (Spring 1956), 187. [CR Aa193]

Bb121 Schwab, Raymond, *Mercure de France*, CCCXXVI, 1111 (1 mars 1956), 560-61. [CR Aa205]

Bb122 Kim, Jean-Jacques, 'Le Testament spirituel de RGL', *La Tour Saint-Jacques*, I, 3 (mars-avr. 1956), 48-62.

Bb123 Gros, Léon-Gabriel, 'Sacre et massacre', *CdS*, XLII, 334 (avr. 1956), 467-71. [CR Aa193, Aa205]

Bb124 Gerald, Jean-Raymond, *Les Lettres et les Arts*, 1 (avr.-mai 1956), 63. [CR Aa205]

Bb125 Silberschlag, Eisig, *Books Abroad* [Norman: Oklahoma], 3 (Summer 1956), 303. [CR Aa205]

Bb126 Lazarus, Maria, 'Ein Dichter', *Antares* [Mainz], IV, 5 (Juli 1956), 28-31. [RD]

1957

Bb127 Laffont-Bompiani, *Dictionnaire des auteurs* (S.E.D.E.S., 1er trim. 1957, 736pp.), 390-91. [RD]

Bb128 Lebois, André, 'Transfiguration du réel dans nos lettres d'aujourd'hui (Promenade anthologique)', *Littérature (Annales publiées par la Faculté de Lettres et de Sciences Humaines de Toulouse)* [Toulouse], 5 (fév. 1957), 21-45. Refs to RD (23, 43-45).

Bb129 Daumal, Véra, introduction to Ab207/Ab209, 269. [Le GJ]

Bb130 Minet, Pierre, 'Contribution au portrait d'un poète', *CdS*, XLIV, 340 (avr. 1957), 387-91.

Bb131 Lecomte, Marcel, 'D'une littérature initiatique', *Synthèses* [Bruxelles], XII, 135-36 (août-sept. 1957), 485-89. Modified version of Bb118. [CR Aa205, Ab207]

Bb132 Sainmont, J.-H., 'Présentation', introduction to Aa208/Aa211, 7-11. [RD, RGL]

1958

Bb133 Nadeau, Maurice, new edition of Bb32 containing Bb45 (Club des Editeurs, coll. 'Hommes et faits de l'Histoire', no.14, 9 jan. 1958,

10176 copies, 340 & xlviiipp.), 123-25 & 139-41. [Le GJ]

Bb134 Boisdeffre, Pierre de, *Une Histoire vivante de la littérature d'aujourd'hui* (Le Livre contemporain, avr. 1958, 768pp.), 326-28. In section 'Aspects d'un nouveau type de roman: l'ésotérisme'. Repr. Bb145, Bb157, Bb161, Bb180, Bb206, Bb270, Bb564.

Bb135 Ribemont-Dessaignes, Georges, *Déjà-Jadis, ou du mouvement Dada à l'espace abstrait* (Julliard, coll. 'Les Lettres Nouvelles', 12 mai 1958, 304pp.). Refs to Le GJ (139-41, 147), RGL (148), RD (156, 177-79). Extract repr. Ba488. Full version repr. Bb371.

Bb136 Boisdeffre, Pierre de, 'En marge d'un numéro spécial d'*Esprit*. Existe-t-il un "Nouveau Roman" français?', *Combat*, 4399 (21 août 1958), 7. [RD]

Bb137 *Anon.*, 'La survie de RD', *Tribune de Lausanne* [Lausanne] (31 août 1958). [CR Aa213]

Bb138 Daumal-Page, Véra, 'Note' (introduction) in Aa213, 7. [RD]

Bb139 Rousseaux, André, 'RD à vingt ans', *Le Figaro Littéraire*, 650 (4 oct. 1958), 2. [CR Aa213]

Bb140 Méautis, Georges, modified version of Bb54 under title 'Le *Voyage du pélerin* et *Le Mont Analogue*'; ch.4 of *Les Pélerinages de l'Ame* (Adyar, 28 nov. 1958 [copyright 1959], 112pp.), 97-110. [RD]

Bb141 Lecomte, Marcel, *Synthèses* [Bruxelles], XIII, 151 (déc. 1958), 273-76. Modified version repr. Bb144. [CR Aa213]

Bb142 K[anters], R[obert], 'La Seconde Génération surréaliste', *L'Express*, 393 (24 déc. 1958), 30. [CR Aa213]

1959

Bb143 Kanters, Robert, 'Il y a trente ans RD', *Actualités Littéraires*, 54 (fév. 1959), 36-37. Includes drawings by RD. [CR Aa213]

Bb144 Lecomte, Marcel, 'L'Expérience spirituelle de RD', *Le Journal des*

Poètes [Dilbeek: Bruxelles], XXIX, 2 (fév. 1959), 2.
Modified version of Bb141. [CR Aa213]

Bb145 Boisdeffre, Pierre de, new edition of Bb134 (Librairie Académique Perrin, fév. 1959, 776pp.), 330-32.
Title of section changes to 'Vers un nouveau type de roman: l'Esotérisme'. [RD]

Bb146 Boisdeffre, Pierre de, 'De Roger Ikor à RD, *Combat*, 4552 (16 fév. 1959), 3. [CR Aa213]

Bb147 *Anon., Bulletin Critique du Livre Français*, 3 (mars 1959), entry 40937, 166-67. [CR Aa213]

Bb148 Roudaut, Jean, 'Sur le chemin de RD', *Critique*, XV, 144 (mai 1959), 400-12. [CR Aa213]

Bb149 T., X., *Etudes*, 303 (juill.-août 1959), 150. [CR Aa213]

Bb150 Lepage, Jacques, 'Un poète de la connaissance', *Marginales* [Bruxelles], 68 (sept.-oct. 1959), 26-32.
Repr. Bb158, Bb159, Bb166. [RD]

Bb151 Toynbee, Philip, 'Holy Mountain', *The Observer* [London], 8781 (18 oct. 1959), 22. [CR At218]

Bb152 Texts in At218.
Contains translation of Bb47.2 and
.1 Shattuck, Roger, 'Introduction', 1-18. Repr. Bb155, Bb219, Bb386, Bb576.1. [RD]

1960

Bb153 Mathias, Pierre, *CdS*, XLIX, 355 (avr.-mai 1960), 477-78. [CR Aa213]

Bb154 Norton, David, 'Return to the heart's longing', *The Nation* [New York], CXCI, 5 (20 Aug. 1960), 95-96. [CR At219]

Bb155 Texts in At219.
Contains Bb152.1 and a translation of Bb47.2. [RD]

Bb156 Picon, Gaëtan, *Panorama de la nouvelle littérature française.*

Introduction, illustrations, documents (Gallimard, *nouvelle édition refondue*, 1960, 678pp.).
Refs to RD & RGL in section 'Accomplissements poétiques. André Breton' (198). Repr. Bb413.

Bb157   Boisdeffre, Pierre de, same as Bb145 (3rd edition, 1960, 804pp.), 330-32. [RD]

1961

Bb158   Lepage, Jacques, same as Bb150, *Courrier des Marches* [Gorbeviller: Meurthe-et-Moselle], 61-62 (print.-été 1961), 24-28. [RD]

Bb159   Lepage, Jacques, same as Bb150, *Esprit*, XXIX, 5 (mai 1961), 1011-17. [RD]

Bb160   Artaud, Antonin, texts in *Œuvres complètes*, vol.2 (Gallimard, nrf, nov. 1961, 289pp.)
Contains Bb21 and
.1   Artaud, Antonin, 'RD (Projet de lettre)', 213-17. [RD]
Volume repr. Bb374.

*Bb160a Pellegrini, Aldo, 'La poesía surrealista', introduction to *Antologia de la poesía surrealista de lengua francesa* (Fabril [Buenos Aires], diciembre 1961). RD & RGL mentioned in section entitled 'Los poetas negros'. Repr. Bb508a.

*Bb160b Lebedev, Jorge, introduction to At220a. [RD]

1962

Bb161   Boisdeffre, Pierre de, same as Bb145 (4th edition, jan. 1962, 804pp.), 330-32. [RD]

Bb162   Burucoa, Christiane, 'RD', *Journal des Poètes* [Dilbeek: Bruxelles], XXXII, 2 (fév. 1962), 2-3. Repr. Bb188.

Bb163   Daumal, Véra, same as Bb47.2 in Aa221. [RD]

Bb164   Girard, Marcel, modified version of Bb70 transferred to section 'Poésie mystique' (Seghers, 26 mars 1962, 352pp.), 231. [RD]

Bb165 Breton, André, same as Bb11, *Manifestes du surréalisme. Edition complète* (Pauvert, 28 mai 1962, 320pp.), 176-77. [RD]

Bb166 Lepage, Jacques, same as Bb150, *Le Bayou* [Houston: Texas], XXVI, 91 (Aut. 1962), 216-221. [RD]

Bb167 Roy, Bruno, introduction to Ab222, 567. [RGL]

Bb168 Billy, André, 'Les propos du samedi', *Le Figaro Littéraire*, 869 (15 déc. 1962), 4. Repr. Ba559. [RGL]

1963

Bb169 Saleck, Maurice, 'Bientôt, au Musée, exposition Sima et de documents consacrés aux poètes du "GJ". Une interview exclusive du romancier Roger Vailland', *L'Union* [Reims], 5630 (4 jan. 1963), 2. [Le GJ]

Bb170 Conil Lacoste, Michel, 'Au Musée de Reims. Joseph Sima et le "GJ"', *Le Monde*, 5618 (8 fév. 1963), 9.

Bb171 Lapouge, Gilles, 'Joseph Sima peintre du "GJ"', *Le Figaro Littéraire*, 878 (16 fév. 1963), 18.

Bb172 Henric, J., 'Sima et les poètes du "GJ"', *Les Lettres Françaises*, 966 (21 fév. 1963), 9.

Bb173 Minet, Pierre, 'Consécration d'un poète,' *NRF*, XXI, 124 (1 avr. 1963), 719-20. [RGL]

Bb174 Grenier, Jean, *Entretiens avec dix-sept peintres non-figuratifs* (Calmann-Lévy, 2e trim. 1963, 236pp.), ch. on 'Sima' 163-73. [Le GJ]

1964

Bb175 Masui, Jacques, introduction to As227, 37. [RD]

Bb176 Nimier, Roger, Bb60 and Bb64 in *Accent Grave*, 7-8, no.sp. 'Roger Nimier un an après' (fév. 1964), 137-43. [RD]

Bb177 Nadeau, Maurice, Bb32, Bb45 in *Histoire du surréalisme.*

Documents surréalistes (Seuil, 12 fév. 1964, 528pp.), 111-12 & 123-26 & 287-96. [Le GJ]

Bb178 Pleynet, Marcelin, 'La Pensée contraire', *Tel Quel*, 17 (print. 1964), 55-68. RD discussed 60-73.

Bb179 Haas, Helmuth de, 'Gefäss des Phantastichen und der Poesie: RDs Roman über den Berg, den es nicht gibt', *Die Welt der Literatur* [Hamburg], I, 1 (19 märz 1964), 18. [CR At229]

Bb180 Boisdeffre, Pierre de, same as Bb145 (5th edition, revised, avr. 1964, 870pp.), 390-92. [RD]

Bb181 Noulet, Emilie, same as Bb38 in *Alphabet critique 1924-1964. Tome I (A-C)* (Presses Universitaires de Bruxelles [Bruxelles], 14 avr. 1964, 386pp.), 219-25 (223-24 on RD).

Bb182 Sernet, Claude, introduction to Ab230, 388. [RGL]

1965

Bb183 Nimier, Roger, Bb60 and Bb64 in *Journées de Lecture* (Gallimard, 4 fév. 1965, 280pp.), 111-19. [RD]

Ba184 Biès, Jean, 'Connaissance, Absolu et Révélation chez RD. Etude sur la vie et l'œuvre', Thèse de 3e cycle, Université de Toulouse ([mars] 1965), 230pp.

Bb185 Roudaut, Jean, 'Finir comme un cigare', *Mercure de France* CCCLIV, 1219 (mai 1965), 96-102. [RGL]

Bb186 Biès, Jean, 'Vie et portrait de RD', *Littérature (Annales de la Faculté de Lettres et de Sciences Humaines de Toulouse)* [Toulouse], XII, 3 (nov. 1965), 185-200.

Bb187 Nadeau, Maurice, Bb133 translated as *The History of Surrealism* (Macmillan [New York], translated by Richard Howard, 1965, 352pp.), 143-44 & 155-58. Repr. Bb246. [Le GJ]

1966

Bb188 Burucoa, Christiane, same as Bb162 in *D'Autres Horribles*

Travailleurs (Editions du Beffroi [Millau], jan. 1966, 122pp.), 109-18. [RD]

Bb189 Waldberg, Patrick, 'Joseph Sima ou l'orient de l'œil', preface to catalogue *Joseph Sima. Œuvres anciennes et récentes 1923-1965*, 22 mars-fin avr. 1966 (Le Point Cardinal, mars 1966), 6pp. (unpag.). [Le GJ]

Bb190 Sima, Joseph, 'Le GJ', *XXe Siècle*, 26 (mai 1966), 101-04. Extract repr. Ba488.

Bb191 Random, Michel, 'L'Etre et l'écriture', in *Les Puissances du dedans* (Denoël, 19 sept. 1966, 448pp.), 249-301. [RD]

Bb192 Sernet, Claude, introduction to Aa237, 6pp. (unpag.). Repr. Ba488. [RGL]

1967

Bb193 Briet, Suzanne, 'La Descendance tourmentée de Rimbaud', *La Grive* [Charleville-Mézières], 133 (jan.-mars 1967), 17-18. [CR Bb191]

Bb194 Bodart, Marie-Thérèse, 'Luc Dietrich et les Puissances de Dedans', *Synthèses* [Bruxelles], XXII, 248 (jan. 1967), 108-13. [CR Bb191]

Bb195 Vancrevel, L[aurens].D., 'RGL', *Litterair Paspoort* [Amsterdam], XXII, 204 (Maart 1967), 65. [CR Aa237]

Bb196 *Anon.*, 'Au fil des lettres. Un procès pas comme les autres', *Le Figaro*, 7055 (4 mai 1967), 4. Repr. Ba559. [RGL]

Bb197 Random, Michel, 'RGL. Les lettres françaises en procès contre une gouvernante abusive', *Aux Ecoutes du Monde*, 2234 (11 mai 1967), 34-35.

Bb198 Texts in *Le Monde [des Livres]*, 6966 (7 juin 1967).
　　　.1　Random, Michel, 'En marge d'un procès. RGL et le GJ, II.
　　　.2　[Aragon, Louis], 'Une déclaration d'Aragon', II. Repr. Ba488, Ba559. [RGL]

Ba199 Texts in *La Grive* [Charleville-Mézières], no.sp.'RD', 135-36

(juill.-déc. 1967), 52pp. Ed. Philippe Vaillant.
Contains texts by RD (see Ab238) and:
.1 Dhôtel, André, 'Expériences d'un au-delà', 2-3.
.2 Ribemont-Dessaignes, Georges, 'Souvenirs', 6-7.
.3 V[aillant], Ph[ilippe], 'Chronologie de RD', 8-12.
.4 Lepage, Jacques, 'RD ou l'expérience fondamentale', 14-17.
.5 Minet, Pierre, '[R]D au départ', 18.
.6 Périn, Luc, 'RD potache à Charleville', 19-20. Extract
   repr. Bb549.
.7 *Anon.*, '[R]D et les Ardennes', 22-23.
.8 Random, Michel, 'RGL, RD et le GJ', 29-33.
.9 Biès, Jean, 'RD, témoin de la fin d'un monde', 34-40.
.10 Lecrique, Camille, 'Poésie noire, poésie blanche', 41-44.
.11 Vaillant, Philippe, 'RD écrivain', 45-47.
.12 Daumal, Jack, 'Précisions nécessaires' (interview), 48-49.
.13 Mavel, Gérard, 'Bibliographie de RD', 50.

Bb200 Rugafiori, Claudio, 'Prefazione', in At239, ix-xx. Extract repr.
       Bb328, Ba465.1. [Le GJ]

Bb201 Pierre-Quint, Léon, new edition of Bb12 (Fasquelle, 20 sept. 1967,
       184pp.). RGL mentioned on 7, 23-24.

Ba202 Texts in *Hermès* [Bruxelles], no.sp. 'La Voie de RD, du GJ au
       Mont Analogue', 5 (1967-1968 [4e trim. 1967]), 138pp. Ed.
       Jacques Masui.
       Contains texts by RD (see Ab242) and
       .1 *Anon.*, 'Pourquoi RD?', 5-10.
       .2 Random, Michel, 'RD et le GJ', 15-27.
       .3 Biès, Jean, 'RD et l'Expérience Gurdjieff', 35-47.
       .4 Masui, Jacques, 'L'Expérience spirituelle de [R]D et l'Inde',
          56-67.
       .5 Richer, Jean, 'Sur le Sentier de la Montagne: RD, conteur',
          87-97.
       .6 Roudaut, Jean, 'L'Attitude poétique de RD', 98-104.
       .7 Minet, Pierre, 'Sur RD', 105-07.
       .8 Christoflour, Raymond, 'Souvenir de RD', 108-11.

Bb203 Etiemble, René, 'RD: *Le Mont Analogue*', in *C'est le bouquet.*
       Hygiène des Lettres. 5 (1940-1967) (Gallimard, nrf, 18 oct. 1967,
       456pp.), 375-80.

Ba204 Biès, Jean, *RD* (Seghers, coll. Poètes d'aujourd'hui, no. 169,
       30 oct. 1967, 196pp.). Repr. Ba376.

Bb205 Dhainaut, Pierre, *Cahiers Internationaux de Symbolisme* [Havré-les-Mons: Belgique], 15-16 (1967-1968), 119. [CR Ab240]

1968

Bb206 Boisdeffre, Pierre de, same as Bb145 (7th edition, newly revised, 1er trim. 1968, 1104pp.), 458-60. [RD]

Bb207 Lambilliotte, Maurice, *Synthèses* [Bruxelles], XXIII, 260 (fév. 1968), 101-02. [CR Ab242]

Bb208 *Anon.*, *Les Lettres Françaises*, 1222 (21 fév. 1968), 13. [CR Ab238, Ab240]

Bb209 Random, Michel, 'L'Univers de RD', *Les Cahiers Littéraires de l'O.R.T.F.*, VI, 11 (25 fév. 1968), 19-22. Introduction to programme on France-Culture 3 mars & 10 mars, 22h 20.

Bb210 Random, Michel, 'Pour une révolution métaphysique. RD et le "GJ"', *Les Nouvelles Littéraires*, 2113 (29 fév. 1968), 3.

Bb211 Hallier, Jean-Edern, 'Un numero RD', *Magazine Littéraire*, 16 (mars 1968), 28-29. [CR Ab242]

Bb212 Plazy, G., 'Le Retour de RD', *Combat*, 7354 (6 mars 1968), 15.

Bb213 Kanters, Robert, 'La Voie de RD', *Le Figaro Littéraire*, 1143 (11 mars 1968), 15-16. [CR Ab240, Ab242]

Bb214 *Anon.*, *Bulletin Critique du Livre Français*, XXIII, 4 (avr. 1968), entry 73044, 275. [CR Ab240]

Bb215 Lobet, Marcel, 'L'Expérience spirituelle de RD', *Revue Générale Belge* [Liège], 4 (avr. 1968), 79-85.

Bb216 Dalmas, André, *La Tribune des Nations*, 1169 (12 avr. 1968), 4. [Le GJ, RD]

Bb217 Texts in *Le Monde [des Livres]*, 7232 (13 avr. 1968), IV-V.
    .1 Dalmas, André, 'Etude', IV. [Le GJ, RD]
    .2 Etiemble, [René], '*La Grande Beuverie*', IV.
    .3 Dhôtel, André, '*Le Mont Analogue*', V.
    .4 Paulhan, Jean, 'RGL ou la passion du risque', V.
    Repr. Bb423, Ba488.
    .5 *Anon.*, 'Pour mieux connaître RD', V.

Bb218 Dhôtel, André, [et al], 'Entretiens du polyèdre. L'Itinéraire spirituel et littéraire de RD', *Etudes*, CCCXXVIII, 328 (mai 1968), 701-23.

Bb219 Texts in At249. Contains Bb152.1 and a translation of Bb47.2. [RD]

Bb220 Bodart, Marie-Thérèse, 'RD: du surréalisme au cristal de la dernière stabilité', *Synthèses* [Bruxelles], XXIII, 263-64 (mai-juin 1968), 115-21.

Bb221 Matthews, J.H., *Books Abroad* [Norman: Oklahoma], XLII, 3 (Summer 1968), 394. [CR Ab240]

Bb222 Attal, Jean-Pierre, 'RD et le "véritable mode d'emploi de la parole"', *Critique*, XXIV, 253 (juin 1968), 558-68. Repr. Bb265.

Bb223 Ayguesparse, Albert, *Marginales* [Bruxelles], 121 (juill. 1968), 96. [CR Ab240]

Bb224 Biès, Jean, 'RD' in *Littérature de notre temps*, vol. 3 (Casterman [Tournai], juill. 1968, 256pp.), 65-68.

Bb225 Texts in At250. Contains translation of Bb47.2 (abr.) and
.1 Rugafiori, Claudio, 'Di una certezza', 143-182. [RD]

Bb226 Texts in At251.
.1 Rugafiori, Claudio, 'Avvertenza', ix-x. [RD]
.2 Masui, Jacques, 'Premessa di Jacques Masui', 5-8. [RD]

Bb227 Daumal, Véra, same as Bb47.2 in Aa252. [RD]

Bb228 Juin, Hubert, 'Les Voyageurs de "l'impossible"', *Les Lettres Françaises*, 1245 (21 août 1968), 4. Repr. Bb337. [RD]

Bb229 Fouchet, Max-Pol, *Un jour, je m'en souviens...Mémoire parleé* (Mercure de France, 21 août 1968, 246pp.).
Refs to RD (68, 80-86, 97).

Bb230 Mauriac, Claude, 'RD, du surréalisme métaphysique à la conquête de l'absolu', *Le Figaro*, 7462 (26 août 1968), 9. [CR Aa244, Aa252]

Bb231 Jans, Adrien, 'On redécouvre RD', *Le Soir* [Bruxelles], 201 (28 août 1968), 22. [CR Aa244, Aa252]

Bb232 Nadeau, Maurice, 'L'Itinéraire de RD', *La Quinzaine Littéraire*, 56 (1 sept. 1968), 3-5.

Bb233 Revel, Jean-François, 'La Caverne surréaliste', *L'Express*, 896 (9 sept. 1968), 63. Repr. Bb237. [RD]

Bb234 Adamov, Arthur, *L'Homme et l'enfant. Journal* (Gallimard, nrf, 20 sept. 1968, 252pp.).
Refs to RGL (31, 61-62, 74-77). Repr. Ba559.

Bb235 Girard, Marcel, same as Bb164 (Seghers, 4e trim. 1968, 408pp.), 234. [RD]

Bb236 [Morvan, J.-B.], *Points et Contrepoints*, 87 (oct. 1968), 52-53. [CR Ab240]

Bb237 Revel, Jean-François, 'Ritornano RD e il "GJ". Platone con la scimmia sulle spalle', *La Fiera Letteraria* [Roma], XLIII, 40 (3 ott. 1968), 21-22.
Modified and translated version of Bb233.

Bb238 Coudert, Marie-Louise, *Europe*, 475-76 (nov.-déc. 1968), 357-58. [CR Aa244. Aa252]

Ba239 *Le Grand Jeu (ré-édition intégrale). Cahiers de l'Herne. L'écriture des vivants, 2* (Minard, 18 nov. 1968, 254pp.). Ed. Marc Thivolet. Contains the three issues of *Le GJ*, with several texts by RD destined for the fourth issue (see Ab254), and:
   .1 Thivolet, Marc, 'Présence du GJ', 20-36. Extract repr. Ba488.
   .2 Minet, Pierre, 'Récit d'un témoin', 226-33.
   .3 Masui, Jacques, 'RD et la Révolte permanente', 234-36.
   .4 Thivolet, Marc, 'Carlo Suarès ou l'anti-Faust', 237-41.
   .5 *Anon.*, 'Chronologie du GJ', 246-49.

Bb240 Hurtin, J., *Magazine Littéraire*, 24 (déc. 1968), 34-37. [CR Ab254]

Bb241 Šmekjal, František, 'Le GJ de J. Sima', *Opus International*, 9 (déc. 1968), 22-26. [Le GJ]

Bb242 Picon, Gaëtan, 'Les formes de l'esprit: Sima et l'état de grâce', *Le Monde*, 7431 (4 déc. 1968), 17. [RD, RGL]

Bb243 Vailland, Roger, *Ecrits intimes* (Gallimard, nrf, 11 déc. 1968, 840pp.).

Contains letters to RD & RGL (32-40) and refs to RD, RGL & Le GJ (84, 97, 104-05, 497-500, 659, 767-68, 774, 827, 834); extracts repr. Ba488. Also contains
.1   Recanati, Jean, introduction to section 1923-1934, 11-21.
[Le GJ]

Bb244   Lamarre, Hugues, 'Au Tribunal de Reims. Bataille juridique autour de 90 lettres inédites du poète visionnaire RGL', *L'Union* [Reims], 7460 (21-22 déc. 1968), 9.

Bb245   Pellus, Daniel, 'Un procès littéraire qui fera jurisprudence', *Le Figaro*, 7565 (25 déc. 1968), 8. [RGL]

Bb246   Nadeau, Maurice, same as Bb187 (Jonathan Cape [London], 1968, 352pp.), 143-44 & 155-58. [Le GJ]

1969

Bb247   *Anon.*, 'Actualité de RD', *La Grive* [Charleville-Mézières], 141 (1er trim. 1969), 30. [CR Ab254]

Bb248   Masui, Jacques, 'Poésie et négation chez RD', *Hermès* [Bruxelles], no.sp. 'Le Vide. Expérience spirituelle en Occident et en Orient', 6 ([1er trim. 1969]), 247-52.

Bb249   Bodart, Marie-Thérèse, *Synthèses* [Bruxelles], XXIV, 271-72 (jan.-fév. 1969), 110-15. [CR Ab254]

Bb250   Lamarre, Hugues, 'M. Malraux gagne seul son procès contre Mme Urbain. Le Tribunal de Reims autorise la publication de la correspondance posthume du poète RGL', *L'Union* [Reims], 7475 (10 jan. 1969), 5.

Bb251   Texts in *Le Monde [des Livres]*, 7464 (11 jan. 1969).
.1   Thivolet, Marc, 'Une réédition: Le GJ', II. Interview with Raphaël Sorin.
.2   *Anon.*, 'Feu vert pour la publication de la correspondance de RGL', II.

Bb252   Le Clec'h, Guy, 'Les lettres de RGL ne sont plus "interdites au public"', *Le Figaro Littéraire*, 1185 (20 jan. 1969), 24-25.

Bb253 Minet, Pierre & Sorin, Raphaël, 'Correspondance : à propos du "GJ"', *Le Monde [des Livres]*, 7476 (25 jan. 1969), III.

Bb254 Pauwels, Louis, 'RD soldat du Je', *Le Nouveau Planète*, 4 (fév. 1969), 51-52. Introduction to Ab259.

Bb255 La Charité, Virginia A., *The Modern Language Journal* [Wisconsin], LIII, 3 (March 1969), 215. [CR Ab240]

Bb256 *Anon.*, 'The real surrealists?', *The Times Literary Supplement* [London], 3498 (13 March 1969), 273. [CR Ab254]

Bb257 Mauriac, Claude, 'RD', in *L'Alittérature contemporaine* (Albin Michel, 18 avr. 1969, 384pp.), 193-99.

Bb258 Audejean, Christian, *Esprit*, 5 (mai 1969), 973-75. [CR Ab254]

Bb259 Perniola, Mario, *Rivista di Estetica* [Torino], XIV, 2 (maggio-agosto 1969), 290-92. [CR At239]

Bb260 Adamov, Arthur, same as Bb36 in *Je...ils. Récits* (Gallimard, nrf, 2 mai 1969, 240pp.).
RGL mentioned on 15 & 82.

Bb261 Landon, Rosemary, 'A statistical study of the vocabulary of six poetic collections of the surrealist period', Ph.D Thesis, Indiana University (June 1969), 232pp.
Includes work on Aa99.

Ba262 Feuillette, Christian-Paul, 'Le cercle et ses métamorphoses dans *Le Mont Analogue*', Maîtrise, Université de Paris (Nanterre) (juin 1969), v & 77pp.

Ba263 Melrose, Robin, '[R]D romancier. Essai d'interprétation de *La Grande Beuverie* et du *Mont Analogue*', M.A. Thesis, University of New South Wales (25 August 1969), 153pp.

Bb264 Henry, Maurice, interview, *Chroniques de l'Art Vivant*, 4 (sept.-oct. 1969), 30-31. [Le GJ]

Bb265 Attal, Jean-Pierre, same as Bb222 in *L'Image "métaphysique" et autres essais* (Gallimard, 25 sept. 1969, 472pp.), 373-83. [RD]

Bb266   Bernard, Michel, 'La littérature et la drogue: qui parle, qui se tait?', *Magazine Littéraire*, 34 (nov. 1969), 13-14. [RD, RGL]

Bb267   Texts in *NRF*, XXXIV, 203 (1 nov. 1969).
.1   Minet, Pierre, 'L'amitié, la jeunesse et la mort', 682-94. Repr. Bb320. [RGL]
.2   Boully, Monny de, 'Les entretiens de Monny de Boully' [with Michel Random] , 702-17. Extract repr. Ba488. [Le GJ, RD, RGL]

Bb268   Minet, Pierre, *Gazette de Lausanne [Littéraire]* [Lausanne], 279 (29 nov. 1969), 1p.(unpag. [10]). [RGL]

Bb269   D[aumal], J[ack], 'Introduction', to Aa261, 9-12. Also includes introduction to the essay (15-16) and commentaries in the section 'Documents' (169-253). [RD]

Bb270   Boisdeffre, Pierre de, Bb145 (abr.) in *Abrégé d'une Histoire vivante de la littérature d'aujourd'hui* (Union Générale d'Editions, 2 vols, coll. '10/18', nos. 424-25, 1969, 768pp.), 320-21. In section 'Un roman de recherche'. [RD]

Bb271   Breton, André, same as Bb51, *nouvelle édition revue et corrigée.* (Gallimard, nrf, coll. 'Idées', no. 284, 1969, 320pp.), 150. This edition repr. Bb366. [Le GJ]

1970

Bb272   Nadeau, Maurice, same as Bb32, new edition (Seuil, coll. 'Points', no.1, 1er trim. 1970, 192pp.), 107-08 & 120-23. [Le GJ]

Bb273   Masui, Jacques, 'Préface (ou: Introduction)' [*sic*] to Aa265, 7-12. [RD]

Bb274   S[medt], M[arc] de, 'RD s'adresse à ces hommes que nous ne verrons jamais', *Le Nouveau Planète*, 15 (mars-avr. 1970), 153. [CR Aa261]

Bb275   Guilleminault, Gilbert, & Bernet, Philippe, *Les Princes des Années Folles* (Plon, 23 avr. 1970, 454pp.). Refs to RD & Le GJ (14, 140-47).

Bb276   Angenot, Marc, 'Discordance, image, métaphore', *Revue de l'Université de Bruxelles* [Bruxelles], 4 (mai-juill. 1970), 359-69. [RD]

Bb277 Bodart, Marie-Thérèse, *Synthèses* [Bruxelles], XXV, 287 (mai 1970), 102-05. [CR Aa265]

Bb278 Bars, Henry, 'Sur la condition des poètes', *La Croix*, 26564 (10 mai 1970), 8. [RD]

Bb279 Greiner, Mechtilt Meijer, 'De andere wereld van Le GJ' [The Other World of Le GJ], *Het Parool* [Amsterdam] (6 Juni 1970), 8. [Le GJ]

Bb280 Simon, Emile, *Jeune Afrique* [Tunis], 492 (9 juin 1970], 6-7. [CR Aa265]

Bb281 C. A., *Gazette de Lausanne [Littéraire]* [Lausanne], 195 (22 août 1970), 1p. (unpag.[6]). [CR Aa265]

Bb282 Gugliemi, Joseph, 'Un monument de mots', *Les Lettres Françaises*, 1348 (26 août 1970), 20-21. [CR Aa265]

Ba283 Random, Michel, *Le GJ* (Denoël, 15 sept. 1970). Vol. 1: *Essai*, 264pp.; vol. 2: *Textes essentiels et documents*, 215pp. The latter contains Bb8 and substantial extracts from Bb9. The former contains
        .1 Lecomte, Edmond, Letter to René Maublanc (extract), 33-34. Complete version repr. Ba559. [RGL]

Bb284 Random, Michel, 'Les Phrères [*sic*] simplistes ou les jeux avant le GJ', *Le Figaro Littéraire*, 1271 (28 sept. 1970), 16-17. Extracts from Ba283, vol. 2 (19-22, 23-24, 26-28).

Bb285 Boyer, Philippe, 'GJ', *Change*, 7, 'Le groupe, la rupture' (4e trim. 1970), 152-61. Repr. Bb375.

Bb286 Baron, Jacques, section on Le GJ in 'Le surréalisme', in *La Littérature* (Centre d'étude et de promotion de la lecture, coll. 'Les Dictionnaires du savoir moderne', 4e trim. 1970, 545pp.), 479-80.

Ba287 Achirian, Josiane, 'Voies et perspectives de la création poétique chez RD', Maîtrise, Université de Paris (Nanterre) (oct. 1970) viii & 95pp.

Bb288 Texts in Aa271.
        .1 Rugafiori, Claudio, 'Préface', 7-16. [RD]

.2 Rugafiori, Claudio, 'La vie et l'œuvre de RD', 245-47.

Bb289 Mauriac, Claude, 'Les écrivains du lundi', *Le Figaro*, 8116
(19 oct. 1970), 19. [CR Ba283]

Bb290 L[oiseau], M[artin], 'Le Retour du GJ', *Magazine Littéraire*, 46
(nov. 1970), 24. [CR Ba283]

Bb291 Galey, Mathieu, 'A la vie à la mort', *L'Express*, 1008 (2 nov.
1970), 66-67. [CR Ba283]

Bb292 Minet, Pierre, & Random, Michel, 'Vos Phrères [*sic*] étaient trop
simplistes (correspondance)', *Le Figaro Littéraire*, 1277
(9 nov. 1970), 24.

Bb293 Brenner, Jacques, '[R]D, [R]GL, Vailland. Connaissez-vous
le GJ?', *Paris-Normandie* [Rouen], 8100 (13 nov. 1970), 12.
[CR Ba283]

Bb294 Maillet, Christian, *Le Soir* [Bruxelles], 265 (14 nov. 1970), 9.
[CR Aa271]

Bb295 Juin, Hubert, 'Le GJ', *Combat*, 8199 (26 nov. 1970), 18.
[CR Ba283]

Bb296 Cachin, Henri, 'Trois grands poètes du XXe siècle en collection de
poche: Breton, Claudel et [R]D', *France-Soir*, 8202 (28 nov. 1970),
9. [CR Aa271]

Bb297 Tavernier, René, 'René Tavernier vous signale...',
Centre-Dimanche. Le Progrès [St Etienne] (29 nov. 1970).
[CR Ba283]

Bb298 Peyrot, Françoise, 'Le GJ des quatre Phrères [*sic*] simplistes',
Chroniques de l'Art Vivant, 16 (déc. 1970-jan. 1971), 24-25.
[CR Ba283]

Bb299 *Anon.*, *Clés pour le Spectacle* [Bruxelles], 4 (déc. 1970), 25.
[CR Aa271]

Bb300 Pia, Pascal, 'Lumière noire', *Carrefour des Idées, des Arts, des
Lettres, des Sciences*, 1366 (2 déc. 1970), 12-13. [CR Ab254,
Ba283]

Bb301 Rousselot, Jean, 'Jeu dangereux', *Les Nouvelles Littéraires*, 2255 (10 déc. 1970), 3. Repr. Bb326, Bb327. [CR Ba283]

Bb302 B[erthier], Ph[ilippe], *Le Bulletin des Lettres* [Lyon], 323 (15 déc. 1970), 384-85. [CR Ba283]

Bb303 *Anon.*, *La Libre Belgique* [Bruxelles], 352 (18 déc. 1970), 18. [CR Ba283]

Bb304 Kanters, Robert, 'Voulez-vous jouer avec eux?', *Le Figaro Littéraire*, 1283 (21 déc. 1970), 19-20. [CR Ba283, Aa271]

Bb305 *Anon.*, *Tiercé-Soir* [Marseille], 8072 (24 déc. 1970), [9]. Abr. version of Bb306.

Bb306 *Anon.*, *Télérama*, 1093 (27 déc. 1970), 40.
Notice of a television programme called 'Post-scriptum' at 22.35h. on 30 déc. devoted to Le GJ on the occasion of Ba283.
Repr. Bb308.

Bb307 Le Marchand, Jean, 'Les Enfants de Rimbaud', *L'Actualité*, 58 (28 déc. 1970), 32-34. [CR Ba283]

Bb308 *Anon.*, *Le Méridional. La France* [Marseille], 8495 (30 déc. 1970), 15. Same as Bb306.

Bb309 Fournet, Claude & Noël, Bernard, 'Le GJ', *Politique-Hebdo*, 13 (31 déc. 1970), 22.

Bb310 Biès, Jean, 'RD, contestataire', *Littératures (Annales publiées par la Faculté de Lettres et de Sciences Humaines de Toulouse)* [Toulouse], XVII, 2 (1970), 95-110.

1971

Bb311 *Anon.*, *Bulletin Critique du Livre Français*, 301 (jan. 1971), entry 80625, 5. [CR Aa271]

Bb312 Aribaut, Robert, 'Sur mon petit écran', *Le Dépêche du Midi* [Toulouse], 8193 (1 jan. 1971), 11.
[CR of programme referred to in Bb306]

Bb313 Sylvestre, Pierre, '[R]D patascientifique', *F*, [1], no.sp.

'L'inquiétante étrangeté' ([1er trim]), 81-82.

Bb314 Pignarre, R., *Les Livres*, 171 (jan. 1971), 52. [CR Aa265]

Bb315 Brochier, Jean-Jacques, 'Vailland dérange toujours', *Magazine Littéraire*, 48 (jan. 1971), 40. [CR Ba283]

Bb316 Recanati, Jean, *Esquisse pour la psychanalyse d'un libertin: Roger Vailland* (Buchet-Chastel, 10 jan. 1971, 360pp.), 72-91. Extract repr. Ba488. [Le GJ]

Bb317 *Anon.*, 'Poètes sacrés, poètes maudits', *La Libre Belgique* [Bruxelles], 28 (29 jan. 1971), 7. [CR Aa271]

Bb318 Miguel, André, 'André Breton et RD', *Clés pour le Spectacle* [Bruxelles], 6 (fév. 1971), 27. [CR Aa271]

Bb319 Foray, Jean-Michel, 'Littérature', *Reflets de la Vie Lyonnaise et du Sud-Est* [Lyon], 245 (11 fév. 1971), 36. [CR Ba283]

Bb320 Minet, Pierre, same as Bb267.1 under title 'Préface' in Aa280, 9-23. [RGL]

Bb321 *Anon.*, *Gazette de Lausanne [Littéraire]* [Lausanne], 48 (27 fév. 1971), 1p. (unpag. [4]). [CR Aa271]

Bb322 Caramétie, Bernard, *NRF*, XXXVII, 219 (1 mars 1971), 90-92. [CR Ba283]

Bb323 Dussault, Jean-Claude, 'Le grand jeu de l'au-delà', *La Presse* [Montréal], 60 (13 mars 1971), Cahier D. [CR Ba283]

Bb324 *Anon.*, *Bulletin Critique du Livre Français*, 305 (avr. 1971), entry 81370, 376. [CR Ba283]

Bb325 D[urozoi], G[érard], *Le Journal des Poètes* [Dilbeek: Bruxelles], 4 ([avr.] 1971), 6-7. [CR Ba283]

Bb326 Rousselot, Jean, same as Bb301 under title 'La vie littéraire: "Le GJ"' in *La Voix de l'Est* [Granby: Québec], 11 249 (12 avr. 1971).

Bb327 Rousselot, Jean, same as Bb301 under title 'Le GJ' in *Maroc*

Demain [Casablanca], 1114 (24 avr. 1971), 4.

Bb328 Rugafiori, Claudio, same as Bb200 under title 'Il GJ' in
*Il Novecento letterario francese. Attraverso la critica
italiana* (Edizione scientifiche italiane [Napoli], maggio 1971),
101-09.

Bb329 Mauriac, Claude, 'RGL aux frontières de l'impossible',
Le Figaro [Littéraire], 1303 (7 mai 1971), III. [CR Aa280]

Bb330 *Anon.*, *Bulletin Critique du Livre Français*, 306 (juin 1971),
entry 81891, 650. [CR Aa280]

Ba331 Agasse, Jean-Michel, 'Poétique/[R]D', Thèse de 3e cycle,
Université de Paris (Nanterre) (18 juin 1971), vol.1, 158pp.
& vol.2, 131pp.
Modified version of ch.3 repr. Ba512.3.

Bb332 Minet, Pierre, 'Autour de la correspondance de RGL.
L'esprit de négation', *Gazette de Lausanne [Littéraire]*
[Lausanne], 140 (19 juin 1971), 1p. (unpag. [3]).

Bb333 Hainaux, René, *International Theatre Information* [Bruxelles]
(aut. 1971), 35. [CR Aa265]

Bb334 Texts in *La Grive* [Charleville-Mézières], XLIV, 152 (4e trim. 1971).
   .1 Germain, Gabriel, '*Nihil intentatum*, tout essayer',
      23-27. [RD]
   .2 Biès, Jean, 'RD et nous', 32-35.

Bb335 Defourny, Michel, 'Des Phrères [*sic*] simplistes au GJ. Une
page d'histoire littéraire', *Marche Romane* [Liège], XXI,
4 (4e trim. 1971), 37-43.

Ba336 Cettour, Françoise, 'Le Rire chez RD', Maîtrise, Université
de Paris (Nanterre) (oct. 1971), [ii] & 59pp.

Bb337 Juin, Hubert, same as Bb228 in *L'Usage de la critique*
(André de Rache [Bruxelles], coll. 'Mains et chemins',
no.2, oct. 1971, 240pp.), 141-45. [RD]

Bb338 Parisse, Jacques, *La Wallonie* [Liège], (15 oct. 1971). [CR Aa280]

Bb339 Noël, Bernard, 'RGL et le "GJ"', *La Quinzaine Littéraire*, 127 (16 oct. 1971), 12-14. [CR Ba283, Aa280]

Bb340 Pignarre, R., *Les Livres*, 178 (nov. 1971), 55. [CR Aa271]

Bb341 Short, R[obert] S[tuart], *Journal of European Studies* [London], I, 4 (Dec. 1971), 383-84. [CR Aa280]

Bb342 Descazaux, P., *Les Livres*, 179 (déc. 1971), 58. [CR Aa280]

Bb343 Abastado, Claude, *Introduction au surréalisme* (Bordas, coll. 'Etudes', no.40, 10 déc. 1971, 254pp.).
Refs to RD & RGL (36), RD (187-88), RGL (191-92).
Modified version repr. Bb405.

Bb344 Noël, Bernard, 'La mort, le mot et le mort-mot', preface to Aa283, 11-19.
Extract repr. Ba488. Full version repr. Bb392. [RGL]

Bb345 Forestier, Louis, *Arthur Rimbaud, I (1972). Images et témoins. (La Revue des Lettres Modernes)*, 323-26 (1971) 129-30. [CR Aa283]

Bb346 Pouilliart, Raymond, 'Théâtre hindou', *Cahiers Théâtre Louvain*, [Louvain], 10-11 ([1971]), 101-02. [CR Aa265]

Ba347 Lepage, Jacques, '"L'asphyxie et l'évidence absurde" de RD', *Courrier du Centre International d'Etudes Poétiques* [Bruxelles], 85 (1971), 20pp. (3-18).

1972

Bb348 Roudaut, Jean, 'Vue d'ensemble. Le GJ poétique', *Critique*, XXVIII, 296 (jan. 1972), 83-91. [CR Ab254, Aa261, Aa265, Aa271, Aa280, Ba283, Ba347]

Bb349 Caramétie, Bernard, *NRF*, XXXIX, 229 (1 jan. 1972), 80-81. [CR Aa280]

Bb350 Pia, Pascal, 'Le Rêve et la vie', *Carrefour*, 1424 (12 jan. 1972), 16-17. [CR Aa280]

Bb351   Rugafiori, Claudio, 'Avvertenza', in At284, ix-xiii. [RD]

Bb352   Rugafiori, Claudio, introduction to Aa287, 5-6. [RD]

Bb353   Rugafiori, Claudio, introduction to Aa288, 5-6. [RD]

Bb354   Angenot, Marc, 'Le surréalisme "noir"', *Les Lettres Romanes* [Louvain], XXVI, 2 (mai 1972), 181-93.
Refs to RGL (190) & RD (191).

Bb355   Mauriac, Claude, 'L'au-delà dans sa réalité même', *Le Figaro [Littéraire]*, 1355 (6 mai 1972), II.
[CR Aa287, Aa288]

Bb356   Jean-Nesmy, Dom Claude, 'Le GJ: Art poétique ou quête spirituelle', *Les Nouvelles Littéraires*, 2332 (5 juin 1972), 7.

Bb357   Thirion, André, *Révolutionnaires sans révolution* (Laffont, 12 juin 1972, 584pp.).
Refs to Le GJ, RD & RGL (146, 181-90, 203-04, 210, 268, 352). Repr. Bb404, Bb415.

Bb358   *Anon.*, *La Libre Belgique* [Bruxelles], 180 (28 juin 1972), 20.
RD referred to as Jean Daumal. [CR Aa287, Aa288]

Bb359   *Anon.*, *Bulletin Critique du Livre Français*, XXVII, 319 (juill. 1972), entry 85070, 900. [CR Aa287, Aa288]

Bb360   K[uffer], J[ean]-L[ouis], *Tribune de Lausanne* [Lausanne], 253 (9 sept. 1972), 17. [CR Aa287, Aa288]

Bb361   Berchan, Richard, *French Review* [Champaign: Illinois], XLVI, 1 (Oct. 1972), 204-06. [CR Aa287, Aa288]

Bb362   Masui, Jacques, 'A propos de RD', *Courrier du Centre International d'Etudes Poétiques* [Bruxelles], 88 (1972), 19-20.

Bb363   Daumal, Véra, same as Bb47.2 in Aa290. [RD]

1973

Bb364   Texts in *Les Cahiers de l'Herméneutique*, 1 (1er trim. 1973).
.1   Minet, Pierre, 'Deux poètes de la connaissance', 13-16. [RGL, RD]

.2   Bazan, Paul, 54-55. [CR Bb191, Aa288]

Bb365   Abellio, Raymond, *Dans une âme et dans un corps (Journal 1971)*
(Gallimard, nrf, 1 fév. 1973, 280pp.).
Refs to Le GJ (74-75), RD (17, 75-76, 235), RGL (235).

Bb366   Breton, André, re-edition of Bb271, 21 fév. 1973. [Le GJ]

Bb367   Mertens, Pierre, 'RD, alpiniste de l'esprit', *Le Soir* [Bruxelles],
73 (28 mars 1973), 26. [CR Aa287, Aa288]

Bb368   Ballerini, Michel, *Le Roman de Montagne en France*
(Arthaud [Grenoble], coll. 'Sempervivum', no.53, 10 avr. 1973,
328pp.).
Ch.5 ('Les nouvelles tendances depuis 1945'), section 7
('Roman policier et roman d'anticipation'), 171-73 on Aa180.

Bb369   Minet, Pierre, same as Bb40, second edition (Editions Jacques
Antoine [Bruxelles], 13 avr. 1973, 278pp.).
Same pagination for refs as first edition. [RGL, RD, Le GJ]

Bb370   Nelson, Hilda, *French Review* [Champaign: Illinois], XLVI,
6 (May 1973), 1247-48. [CR Ba283]

Bb371   Ribemont-Dessaignes, Georges, same as Bb135, new edition
(Union Générale d'Editions, coll. '10/18', no.795, 8 juin 1973,
448pp.).
Refs to Le GJ (202-06, 215), RGL (216), RD (229, 258-62).

Bb372   Benoist, Luc, 'Eurythmie et spiritualité', *Etudes Traditionnelles*,
439 (sept.-oct. 1973), 200-06. [RD]

Bb373   Biès, Jean, 'RD' (ch.3) in *Littérature française et pensée
hindoue des origines à 1950* (Klincksieck, 4e trim. 1973
[copyright 1974], 684pp.), 491-560.

Bb374   Artaud, Antonin, same as Bb160 (*nouvelle édition revue
et augmentée*, 15 nov. 1973, 368pp.).

Bb375   Boyer, Philippe, same as Bb285 in *L'écarté(e) (fiction
théorique)* (Seghers/Laffont, coll. 'Change', 19 nov. 1973,
368pp.), 47-57. [Le GJ]

Ba376 Biès, Jean, same as Ba204 (second edition, 1973, 189pp.). [RD]

Bb377 Solmi, Sergio, introduction to At295, 76-77. [RD]

1974

Bb378 Texts in Aa301.
    .1 Minet, Pierre, 'Avant-propos', 7-8. [RGL]
    .2 Thivolet, Marc, 'Le sang, le sens et l'absence' [introduction], 9-27. [RGL]

Bb379 Benoist, Luc, *Etudes Traditionnelles*, 446 (nov.-déc. 1974), 284-86. [CR Ba376]

Bb380 Mauriac, Claude, 'Il y a encore des poètes maudits', *Le Figaro*, 9306 (22 nov. 1974), 26. [CR Aa301]

Bb381 Giroud, Michel, *Art Vivant*, 54 (déc. 1974-jan. 1975), 38-39. [CR Aa301]

Bb382 Kanters, Robert, 'Faites votre grand jeu rien ne va plus', *Le Figaro [Littéraire]*, 1490 (7 déc. 1974), III. [CR Aa301]

Bb383 Bott, François, 'RGL: un rire désespéré', *Le Monde [des Livres]*, 9315 (27 déc. 1974), 9.
Extract repr. Ba488. [CR Aa301]

Bb384 Givone, Sergio, *Hybris e melancholia. Studi sulle poetiche del Novecento* (U. Mursia [Milano], coll. 'Saggi di Estetica e di Poetica', no.19, 1974, 180pp.).
Ch.3 ('Surrealismo e misticismo'), part 1 ('I fatti e il problema'), 139-42 & part 2 ('Il "GJ": l'ascesi'), 147-53. [Le GJ]

Bb385 Linhartová, Věra, *Joseph Sima, ses amis, ses contemporains* (La Connaissance [Bruxelles], coll. 'Témoins et témoignages (Monographies)', 1974, 149pp.).
Ch.3 ('Autour du GJ'), 33-41 & ch.5 ('Le monde analogue'), 66-70. Extract repr. Ba488. [RD, RGL]

Bb386 Texts in At300.
Contains translation of Bb47.2, Bb152.1 (with the addition of a postscript written in 1974), and
    .1 Needham, Jacob, 'Foreword', 7-12. [RD]

1975

Bb387   Vier, Jacques, 'RD', *Francia* [Napoli], III,
13 (genn.-marzo 1975), 68.
In section 'Portraits de poètes'.

Bb388   Oster, Daniel, 'Le casse-dogme', *Les Nouvelles Littéraires*,
2467 (6 jan. 1975), 4. [CR Aa301]

Bb389   Alexandrian, Sarane, *Le Surréalisme et le rêve* (Gallimard,
nrf, coll. 'Connaissance de l'Inconscient', 14 jan. 1975,
510pp.), 471-75 (in ch.XI 'Les ennemis du dedans'). [Le GJ]

Bb390   Begot, Jean-Pierre, 'Premier tome de ses œuvres complètes:
RGL, ou "l'agonie métaphysique"', *Le Quotidien de Paris*,
244 (15 jan. 1975), 11. [CR Aa301]

Bb391   *Anon.*, *L'Imprévu*, 5 (31 jan. 1975), 13. [CR Aa301]

Bb392   Noël, Bernard, same as Bb344 in *Treize cases du je. Journal*
(Flammarion, coll. 'Textes', 28 fév. 1975, 294pp.), 9-14. [RGL]

Bb393   Merlin, Irène, *Exit*, 5 (print. 1975), 88-89. [CR Aa301]

Bb394   K[uffer], J[ean]-[Louis], *La Liberté* [Fribourg]
(1 mars 1975). [CR Aa301]

Bb395   Miguel, André, 'Culture bourgeoise et culture de masse',
Clés [Bruxelles], 4 (avr. 1975), 28-29. [CR Aa301]

Bb396   *Anon.*, *Bulletin Critique du Livre Français*, 353 (mai 1975),
entry 93077, 620. [CR Aa301]

Bb397   N., Ch., 'RGL', *Cahiers Bleus*, 1 (été 1975), 98.

Ba398   Knight, Kelton Wallace, 'Death as a metaphor for being in
the works of RD', Ph.D., University of Utah (June 1975), 162pp.

Bb399   Bertozzi, G[abriele]-A[ldo], 'Introduzione', in At305,
v-xv. [Le GJ, RGL]

Bb400   Pouilliart, Raymond, *Centre d'Action Culturelle de la
Communauté d'Expression Française* [Namur: Belgique], 30
(sept. 1975). [CR Aa301]

Bb400a Nelli, René, *Joë Bousquet: sa vie et son œuvre* (Albin Michel, 2 sept. 1975, 256pp.), 60-65. [Le GJ]

Bb401 G[ateau], J[ean]-C[harles], *NRF*, XLVI, 275 (1 nov. 1975), 75-77. [CR Aa301]

Bb402 Finck, Jeannine, 'Tentatives mystiques de trois poètes incroyants: Breton, [R]D, Bousquet (1920-1940)', Thèse de 3e cycle, Université de Paris VIII (8 nov. 1975), 229 & li pp.

Bb403 Vancrevel, Laurens, 'De mythe van het ware leven' [The Myth of the True Life], *Elseviers Magazine* [Amsterdam] (22 nov. 1975), 137-39. [Le GJ]

Bb404 Thirion, André, same as Bb357 translated as *Revolutionaries without revolution* (Macmillan [New York], 1975, viii & 504pp., translated by Joachim Neugroschel).
Refs to Le GJ, RD, RGL (161-62, 164-70, 183-84, 189). Repr. Bb415.

Bb405 Abastado, Claude, *Le surréalisme* (Hachette, coll. 'Espaces littéraires', 1975, 320pp.).
Refs to Le GJ (21), RD (276-77), RGL (279-80). The last two refs are the same as in Bb343.

1976

Bb406 K[anceff], E[manuele], *Studi Francesi* [Torino], LVIII, 1 (genn.-apr. 1976), 193. [CR Aa301]

Bb407 Solmi, Sergio, *La Luna di Laforgue e altri scritti di letteratura francese* (Arnoldo Mondadori [Milano], marzo 1976, 286pp.).
Contains '*Una esperienza fondamentale* di RD' (203-23) & '*Lettere* di RD' (256-60).

Bb408 Bruézière, Maurice, 'En marge du surréalisme: Joë Bousquet, RD', in *Histoire descriptive de la littérature contemporaine* (Berger-Levrault, 2e trim. 1976, 382pp.), 38-40.

Bb409 P[ouilliart], R[aymond], *Les Lettres Romanes* [Louvain], XXX, 2 (mai 1976), 189-90. [CR Aa280]

Ba410   Néaumet, Jean, 'RD et l'ésotérisme', Thèse de 3e cycle, Université de Paris IV (4 juin 1976), 248pp.

Bb411   Picard, Michel, *Revue d'Histoire Littéraire de la France*, LXXVI, 4 (juill.-août 1976), 683-85. [CR Aa301]

Bb412   Picon, Gaëtan, *Journal du surréalisme 1919-1939* (Skira [Genève], sept. 1976, 234pp.), 80. [Le GJ]

Bb413   Picon, Gaëtan, same as Bb156, new edition (Gallimard, 1 sept. 1976, 368pp.), 229. [RD, RGL]

Bb414   Bertozzi, G[abriele]-A[ldo], *Rimbaud attraverse i movimenti d'avanguardia* (Luciano Lucarini [Roma], nov. 1976, 164pp.). Ch.3 ('Il ritorno degli "orribili lavoratori"', 97-136), 124-36. [Le GJ]

Bb415   Thirion, André, same as Bb404 (Cassell [London], 1976, same pagination). [Le GJ, RD, RGL]

1977

Bb416   Rugafiori, Claudio, 'Caves en plein ciel', introduction to Aa315, 16pp. (unpag.). [RGL]

Bb417   Brochier, Jean-Jacques, *L'Aventure des surréalistes 1914-1940* (Stock, coll. 'Les Grands Auteurs', 5 jan. 1977, 336pp.), 235-37. [Le GJ]

Bb418   Pasquier, Pierre, 'Le Masque et la Transparence, ou l'Image du Théâtre Oriental en Europe entre 1920 et 1940 (Antonin Artaud, Paul Claudel, Edward Gordon Craig et RD)', Thèse de 3e cycle, Université de Caen (11 fév. 1977), 664pp.

Bb419   Dupuis, Jean-François, *Histoire désinvolte du surréalisme* (Paul Vermont [Nonville; *sic*, in fact Paris], coll. 'Le Rappel au désordre', 15 fév. 1977, 168pp.), 32. [Le GJ]

Bb420   Naville, Pierre, *Le Temps du surréel. L'Espérance mathématique. Tome 1* (Galilée, coll. 'Ecritures/Figures', 2 mai 1977, 336pp.), 291-93. [RD]

Bb421 Lévy, Tony, 'Histoires de nombres. A propos de l'origine des numérations', *Les Temps Modernes*, XXXIII, 373-74 (août-sept. 1977), 298-313. Refs to RD 311-12.

Bb422 Rugafiori, Claudio, 'Avertissement', in Ab308, 1p. (unpag.[v]). [Le GJ]

Bb423 Texts in *Zona Franca* [Caracas: Venezuela], III, 3 (sept.-oct. 1977).
Contains a translation of Bb217.4 under the title 'RGL o la pasión del riesgo', and
.1 O., A., 'RGL (1907-1943) a los setenta años de su nacimiento', 34.

Bb424 Couillard, Viviane, 'Le labyrinthe de *La Grande Beuverie*', *Eidôlon (Cahiers du Laboratoire Pluridisciplinaire de Recherches sur l'Imagination Littéraire. Université de Bordeaux III)* [Bordeaux], 2, no. 'Labyrinthes' (oct. 1977), 121-33. [RD]

Bb425 Laude, André, 'Trois mystiques encanaillés sortent "Le GJ"', *Les Nouvelles Littéraires*, 2607 (20 oct. 1977), 8. [CR Ab308]

Bb426 Texts in *Canal*, 9 (1 nov. 1977).
.1 Maxwell, H.J[osèphe], 'Les rêves révoltés du GJ', 16-17.
.2 *Anon.*, 17. [CR Aa315]

Bb427 Néaumet, Jean, 'RD ou la volonté de connaissance', *Question de*, 21 (nov.-déc. 1977), 64-77.

Bb428 Fauchereau, Serge, 'L'avant-garde d'hier', *La Quinzaine Littéraire*, 266 (1 nov. 1977), 13-14. [CR Ab308]

Bb429 Texts in Aa319.
Contains Bb1, Bb18 and
.1 Minet, Pierre, 'Avant-propos', vii-viii. [RGL]
.2 Bolléry, Jean, 'Présentation', ix-x. [RGL]

Bb430 Péju, Pierre, 'L'Enjeu du GJ. De la révolte absolu à la perte inévitable de soi-même', *Rouge*, 505 (21 nov. 1977), 10-11. [CR Ab308]

Bb431 C[athelin], J., 'RGL [*sic*], GJ', *Le Généraliste*, 90 (déc. 1977), 45. [CR Ab308]

Bb432 François, Bruno, 'RD, du GJ à Gurdjieff', *Magazine Littéraire*, 131 (déc. 1977), 28-29.

Bb433 Texts in *Le Monde [des Livres]*, 10232 (23 déc. 1977).
.1 Mauriac, Claude, 'La métaphysique expérimentale du "GJ"', 15 & 18. Repr. Bb549. [CR Ab308]
.2 Bott, François, 'Les aveux effarés de RGL', 18. [CR Aa319]

Bb434 Lestrient, Eric, 'RD. L'expérience poétique suprême: se détruire', in *Histoire de la littérature française du XXe siècle. Tome III. De l'avant-guerre à l'après-guerre* (Famot [Genève], ed. Jean Dumont, 1977, 472pp.), 377-82.

1978

Bb435 *Anon.*, '[R]GL complété', *Canal*, 12 (jan. 1978), 5. [CR Aa319]

Bb436 Rich, Auguste, & Gaudin, Louis, *La Gazette du Lecteur* [Le Paradou], 2 (jan. 1978), 1p. (unpag.[3]). [CR Aa310]

Bb437 Texts in *Magazine Littéraire*, 132 (jan. 1978).
.1 Minet, Pierre, 'RGL ou le refus d'être', 68-69.
.2 Adamov, Arthur, Letter to P. Minet, 69. Repr. Ba559. [RGL]
.3 Breton, André, Letter to P. Minet, 69 . Repr. Ba488, Ba559. [RGL]

Bb438 Ladouce, Laurent, *Le Nouvel Espoir*, 1 (1 jan. 1978), 25-26. [CR Aa344]

Bb439 A[ccarias], J[ean]-L[ouis], *L'Originel*, 3 (jan.-fév. 1978), 38-39. [CR Ab308]

Bb440 Brincourt, André, 'RD, RGL, les jeux de la nuit', *Le Figaro [Littéraire]*, 57984 (8 jan. 1978), 23. [CR Aa310, Aa319]

Bb441 Clémentin, Jean, 'Tous au refrain: sauvez, sauvez vos âmes au nom du sacré cœur', *Le Canard Enchaîné*, 2985 (11 jan. 1978), 7. [CR Ab308]

Bb442 Pache, Jean, 'Des sentiers tissés de réponses', *24 Heures* [Lausanne] (14 jan. 1978), 37. [CR Aa319]

Bb443 *Anon.*, 'Une nouvelle réalisation des éditions Jean-Michel Place', *Le Nouvel Observateur*, 688 (16 jan. 1978), 13. [CR Ab308]

Bb444 Wandelère, Frédéric, 'Sur quatre recueils de poèmes', *La Liberté* [Fribourg] (28 jan. 1978). [CR Aa319]

Bb445 Texts in *Bulletin Critique du Livre Français*, 386 (fév. 1978).
.1 *Anon.*, entry 102696, 217. [CR Aa310]
.2 *Anon.*, entry 102723, 230. [CR Aa319]

Bb446 Deluy, Henri, *L'Humanité*, 10406 (9 fév. 1978), 10. [CR Aa319]

Bb447 Mottaz, Philippe, 'Subversion en marge du surréalisme. Du GJ et de quelques dandys', *24 Heures* [Lausanne] (20 fév. 1978), 37. [CR Ab308, Aa310, Aa319]

Bb448 Audejean, Christian, *Esprit*, 3 (mars 1978), 109-10. [CR Aa301, Aa319]

Bb449 Béarn, Pierre, *La Passerelle*, 31 (print. 1978), 37. [CR Aa319]

Bb450 Fauchereau, Serge, 'Tzara, RD, RGL', *La Quinzaine Littéraire*, 275 (16 mars 1978), 12. [CR Aa310, Aa319]

Bb451 G., A., *Le Soir* [Bruxelles], 69 (22 mars 1978), 20. [CR Ab308]

Bb452 Gateau, Jean-Charles, 'Le Surréalisme a ses monuments et ses sites classés. Mais aussi ses banlieues et ses terrains vagues', *Gazette de Lausanne* [Lausanne], 70 (25 mars 1978), II. [CR Aa310, Aa319]

Bb453 Delon, Michel, *Europe*, 588 (avr. 1978), 244-45. [CR Aa310]

Bb454 Joulié, Gérard, *La Liberté* [Fribourg] (6-7 mai 1978). [CR Aa310]

Bb455 Maxwell, H.J[osèphe], 'Un momentané avec Harfaux', *Canal*, 17 (15 mai 1978), 11. [Le GJ]

Bb456   Vandewalle, Maurice, *Hors II* [Saint Just en Chaussée], 3-4 ([juin] 1978), 150. [CR Aa310]

Bb457   Juin, Hubert, 'La voix inimitable de RGL', *Magazine Littéraire*, 138 (juin 1978), 65-66.
Extract repr. Ba488. [CR Aa319]

Bb458   Aga-Rossi, Laura, 'Dalla droga alla "conoscenza". Le Regole del Grande Gioco: "Vince chi [*sic*] perde"', *L'Informatore Librario* [Roma], VIII, 7 (luglio 1978), 14-16. [CR Aa310, Aa319]

Bb459   Leuwers, Daniel, *NRF*, LII, 307 (août 1978), 122-24.
[CR Aa310]

Bb460   Brenner, Jacques, 'Le GJ', in *Histoire de la littérature française de 1940 à nos jours* (Fayard, 14 sept. 1978, 588pp.), 113-14.
In section 'Laboratoires secrets'.

Bb461   Texts in *Les Livres*, 240 (oct. 1978).
    .1   Chevallier, J., 76. [CR Aa310]
    .2   Suquet, J., 78. [CR Aa319]

Bb462   Rugafiori, Claudio, introduction to Aa322, 7-12.
Extract repr. Ba488. [RD]

Bb463   Borer, Alain, 'Rimbaud dans le GJ', *Cahiers du Centre Culturel Rimbaud* [Charleville-Mézières], 6 (nov. 1978), 3pp. (unpag.).
Repr. Ba464, Ba551. [Le GJ]

Ba464   Texts in *Cahiers de la Maison de la Culture André Malraux* [Reims], no.sp. 'Actualité du GJ', ed. Jean-Marie le Sidaner (14 nov. 1978), 32pp. (unpag.), 1000 copies.
Contains Bb463 and
    .1   Maxwell, H.J[osèphe], biography of Le GJ, [2-8]
Followed by brief responses to the question 'Existe-t-il une "actualité" du "GJ"?':
    .2   Roudaut, Jean, [12].
    .3   Miguel, André, [13].
    .4   Carn, Hervé, [14].
    .5   Lepage, Jacques, 'A propos du GJ', [15].
    .6   White, Kenneth, 'RD, le GJ et la "poésie blanche"', [16-17].

.7   Dhainaut, Pierre, [18].
.8   Duault, Alain, 'Le GJ aujourd'hui, pour moi', [19].
.9   Durozoi, Gérard, [20-21].
.10 Carassou, Michel, 'L'enjeu du GJ reste actuel', [23].
.11 Lambert, Jean-Clarence, 'Le GJ', [25].
.12 Camus, Michel, 'Le Gardien du seuil', [26-27]. Repr. Ba465.
.13 Juin, Hubert, [28].

Ba465   Texts in *L'Originel*, no.sp. 'Le GJ. Révélation Révolution',
        ed. Jean-Louis Accarias, 7 (déc. [1978]-jan. [1979]).
        Contains Ba464.12, texts by RD & RGL (see Ab324 and
        Ab328) and
        .1   Rugafiori, Claudio, 'Le GJ', 4-7. Extract from Bb200
             translated by H.J[osèphe] Maxwell.
        .2   Maxwell, H.J[osèphe], 'Bergson et le GJ', 8-9. Extract
             repr. Ba488.
        .3   [Lams, Mariane], 'Entretien avec Mariane Lams, par
             Daniel Giraud', 11-12.
        .4   [Ribemont-Dessaignes, Georges], 'Entretien avec G[eorges]
             Ribemont-Dessaignes, par Michel Random', 12-13.
        .5   [Sima, Joseph], 'Entretien avec Joseph Sima, par
             Michel Random', 16-17.
        .6   Accarias, Jean-Louis, '"Révélation-Révolution". Banalités
             de base', 18-22.
        .7   Random, Michel, 'RGL', 23-28. Extract repr. Ba488.
        .8   Agasse, J[ean]-M[ichel], 'RD, la poésie, l'ascèse', 32-36.
        .9   Agasse, J[ean]-M[ichel], 'RD et la pataphysique', 37-38.
        .10 [Boully, Monny de], '[R]D. Entretien avec Monny de
             Boully. Propos recueillis par Michel Random', 38-39.
        .11 Duplessis, Yvonne, 'La vision extra-retinienne. RD
             "sujet" de René Maublanc', 40-42.
        Under title 'Le GJ et le surréalisme', two interviews by
        Michel Random:
        .12 [Ribemont-Dessaignes, Georges], 'Entretien avec Ribemont
             Dessaignes' [*sic*], 43-44.
        .13 [Boully, Monny de], 'Boully, Monny de', 44-45.
        .14 *Anon.*, 'Chronologie du GJ', 49.

Bb466   Leheutre, Claude, 'Le GJ. La poésie conçue et vécue
        comme un risque', *L'Ardennais* [Charleville-Mézières], 10466
        (29 déc. 1978), 19. [CR Ab308]

Bb467   Bernier, Jean, same as Bb17 in *L'Amour de Laure* (Flammarion,
        coll. 'Textes', 1978, 199pp.), 47. [CR *Le GJ* III]

Bb468 *Anon.*, introduction to Aa329, 3pp. (unpag.[3-5]). [RGL]

1979

Bb469 Leuwers, Daniel, *Europe*, 599 (mars 1979), 240. [CR Aa319]

Bb470 Nelson, Hilda, 'Gérard de Nerval and RD, two Nyctalopes', *Nineteenth Century French Studies* [New York], VIII, 3-4 (Spring 1979-Summer 1980), 236-51.

Bb471 Brincourt, André, 'RD', in *Les Ecrivains du XXe siècle. Un musée imaginaire de la littérature mondiale* (Retz, coll. 'Les Encyclopédies du savoir moderne', 2e trim. 1979, 735pp.), 207-10.

Bb472 Texts in *Joseph Sima, 1891-1971, Œuvre graphique et amitiés littéraires* (Bibliothèque Nationale, 22 mai 1979).
    .1 Coron, Antoine, 'Poésie de la peinture, peinture de la poésie', 9-13. [Le GJ]
    .2 Coron, Antoine, 'Joseph Sima et le "GJ"', 41-42.
    .3 Sima, Joseph, Letter to Arthur Adamov dated 25 nov. 1960 (extracts), 47. [RGL]

Bb473 Chénieux-Gendron, Jacqueline, 'Le surréalisme et le roman (1922-1950)', Doctorat d'Etat, Université de Paris (Sorbonne) (26 mai 1979), 4 vols, 913pp.
Part 5 ('Des "ontologies de l'impossible"'), section 3 ('RD: le passage initiatique comme sens'), 691-728. Repr. Bb540 (without section on RD). Many other refs to RD.

Bb474 Richaud, André, 'Faille et faillite chez RGL', *Courrier du Centre International d'Etudes Poétiques* [Bruxelles], 129-31 (sept.-oct. 1979), 41-46.

Bb475 Couillard, V[iviane], 'Le GJ', in *Histoire littéraire de la France. Vol.II, 1913-1939* (Editions Sociales, ed. Pierre Abraham & Roland Desné, 4e trim. 1979, 496pp.), 247-49. Repr. Bb546.

Bb476 Bowie, Malcolm, 'Raising the glass', *The Listener* [London], CII, 2638 (22 nov. 1979), 712-13. [CR At332]

Ba477 Jacques, Chantal, 'Le GJ 1928-1932', Thèse de 3e cycle,

Université de Paris IV (déc. 1979), 260pp.

Bb478 Pasquier, Pierre, 'L'Aurore de la bénédiction, ou RD et la tentation de l'art sacré', *Actes du XVe Congrès de la Société Française de Littérature Générale et Comparée: L'Histoire des Religions dans le Mouvement Symboliste Européen (1880-1930) (Caen 20-22 déc. 1979)* [Caen] (1979), 99-131.

*Bb479 Navarri, Roger, 'La critique surréaliste', Doctorat-ès-Lettres, Université de Paris (1979). Part II, section 3 on RD.

1980

Bb480 Maxwell, H.J[osèphe], 'Présentation', catalogue to the exhibition *Le GJ*, held at the Maison de la Culture du Havre, Jan. 1980 (Maison de la Culture du Havre [Le Havre], jan. 1980, 39pp.), 6pp. (unpag. [2-7]).

Ba481 Guichard, Gérard, 'RD. Langage et connaissance. Recherche d'une poétique', Doctorat d'Etat, Université François Rabelais de Tours (mars 1980), 558pp.

Bb482 Linhartová, Věra, 'Crâne et grotte. Rivières souterraines de Sima', *Cahiers du Musée National d'Art Moderne*, 4 (avr.-juin 1980), 194-205. [RGL, RD]

Bb483 Wood, Michael, 'The Great Game', *New York Review of Books* [New York], XXVII, 6 (17 Apr. 1980), 41-43. [CR At333]

Bb484 Texts in *Dictionnaire des auteurs de langue française* (Garnier, 25 sept. 1980, 440pp.).
 .1 Jourdain, Gabriel & Favre, Yves-Alain, 'RD', 117-18.
 .2 Jourdain, Gabriel & Favre, Yves-Alain, 'RGL', 175.

Bb485 A[ragon], L[ouis] & B[reton], A[ndré], same as Bb9 in *Tracts surréalistes et déclarations collectives. Tome I, 1922-1939* (Le Terrain Vague, oct. 1980, 544pp.), 96-129. [Le GJ]

Bb486 Virmaux, Odette & Virmaux, Alain, introduction to Ab338, 197. [RD]

Bb487 Caws, Mary Ann, 'Dark framing and the analogical ascent', *New York Literary Forum* [New York], 4, no.sp. 'The occult in language and literature' (1980), 147-58. [RD]

1981

Ba488 Virmaux, Alain, & Virmaux, Odette, *RGL et Le GJ* (Belfond, 1er trim. 1981, 283pp.).
Contains Bb30.1, Bb30.2, Bb192, Bb198.2, Bb217.4, Bb437.3, and short extracts from Bb1, Bb13, Bb21, Bb31, Bb119, Bb135, Bb190, Ba239.1, Bb243, Bb267.2, Bb316, Bb344, Bb383, Bb385, Bb457, Bb462, Ba465.2, Ba465.7. Previously unpublished:
  .1 Duflot, Jean, extract from a radio interview with Michel Random (mars 1968), 229.
  .2 Reich, Zdenko, Letter to the authors dated 9 fév. 1981 (extract), 232.
  .3 Puyaubert, Jean, extract from a radio programme 'Hommage à RGL' (29 déc. 1963), 233.
  .4 Chautemps, Jacques, extract from ibid., 234.
  .5 Neveux, Georges, interview with Alain Virmaux, 253-54.
  .6 Legris, Jacques, interview with the authors, 255.
  .7 [*Tribunal de Reims*], 'Extrait du jugement du 9 jan. 1969 rendu par le Tribunal de Grande Instance de Reims au sujet du droit de publier la correspondance de RGL', 257-59. Full version repr. with a commentary in Ba559.

Bb489 Ezine, Jean-Louis, 'L'Avalanche', *Les Nouvelles Littéraires*, 2772 (29 jan. 1981), 3. [CR Aa344]

Bb490 Amette, Jacques-Pierre, 'Ironique', *Le Point*, 438 (9 fév. 1981), 16. [CR Aa344]

Bb491 Rappo, Pierre, *Le Courrier Picard* [Amiens], 11296 (11 fév. 1981), 23. [CR Aa344]

Bb492 *Anon., Révolution*, 51 (20 fév. 1981), 51. [CR Aa344]

Bb493 Varenne, Jean, *Question de*, 41 (mars 1981), 123-25. [CR Aa344]

Bb494 Maxwell, H.J[osèphe] & Rugafiori, Claudio, 'Avant-propos', in Aa344, 7-8. Repr. Bb576. [RD]

Bb495 Farrayre, Jean, 'De l'alpinisme analogique', *Al Maghrib* [Rabat] (22 mars 1981). [CR Aa344]

Bb496 Kanters, Robert, 'Esotérisme et surréalisme', *Mélusine (Cahiers du Centre de Recherches sur le Surréalisme)* [Lausanne], no. 'Occulte-Occultation' (31 mars 1981), 11-21. [Le GJ, RD]

Bb497 Jaubert, Jacques, 'Le dernier voyage de RD', *Lire*, 68 (avr. 1981), 37. [CR Aa344]

Bb498 Descamps, Pierre, *Feuille d'Annonces* [Valenciennes], 6315 (11 avr. 1981), 6. Repr. Bb503. [CR Aa344]

Bb499 Mambrino, Jean, 'Lire comme on se souvient', *Etudes*, CCCLIV, 5 (mai 1981), 654-56. [CR Aa344]

Bb500 Gateau, Jean-Charles, '[R]D partageait avec Artaud l'expérience des limites', *Journal de Genève [Littéraire]* [Genève], 101 (2 mai 1981), IV. [CR Aa344]

Bb501 Brincourt, André, 'Le poète virtuel du GJ', *Le Figaro*, 11419 (22 mai 1981), 21. [CR Ba488]

Bb502 Sorin, Raphaël, 'L'"archange" du GJ', *Le Monde [des Livres]*, 11299 (29 mai 1981), 12. [CR Ba488]

Bb503 Descamps, Pierre, same as Bb498 in *La Gazette de la Région du Nord* [Lille], 4493 (10 juin 1981), 16. [CR Aa344]

Bb504 Virmaux, Odette, & Virmaux, Alain, 'A propos de RGL', *Le Monde [des Livres]*, 11317 (19 juin 1981), 25. Reply to Bb502.

Bb505 Trémolières, François, *NRF*, 342-43 (1 juill.-août 1981), 191-92. [CR Aa344]

Bb506 Bourgeois, Claude, 'L'aventure du GJ', *La Dépêche. La Liberté* [St Etienne] (11 juill. 1981). [CR Ba488]

Bb507 Perros, Georges, same as Bb67 in *Lectures. Comptes rendus et articles critiques* (Le Temps qu'il fait, août 1981), 18-20. [RD]

Bb508 Chavardès, Maurice, 'Mille Miller', *Témoignage Chrétien*, 1938 (31 août 1981), 22. [CR Aa344]

Bb508a Pellegrini, Aldo, same as Bb160a in new edition (Argonauta [Barcelona/Buenos Aires], 360pp.), 13-43.

Bb509 Biès, Jean, 'Le retour à RD', *Aurores*, 16 (sept.-oct. 1981), 4.

Bb510 Z[iegelmeyer], P[ierre], *Plein Chant* [Bassac: Châteauneuf-sur-Charente], 5 (sept.-oct. 1981), 73-74. [CR Aa344]

Bb511 Perrier, Jean-Claude, 'RD: la quête de l'absolu', *Le Quotidien de Paris*, 554 (8 sept. 1981), 32. [CR Aa344]

Ba512 *RD ou le retour à soi (Textes inédits et études)* (L'Originel, 11 sept. 1981, 304pp.). Contains Bb29, texts by RD (see Ab345) and
   .1 Maxwell, H.J[osèphe], 'Brève biographie', 9-13.
   .2 Accarias, Jean-Louis, 'Attitude, degré zéro. Collage pour illustrer l'attitude daumalienne', 99-127.
   .3 Agasse, Jean-Michel, 'L'univers poétique de [R]D ou la réintégration', 129-67. Modified version of Ba331, ch.3 (94-133).
   .4 Maxwell, H.J[osèphe], 'A propos de *La Grande Beuverie'*, 169-88.
   .5 Néaumet, Jean, 'RD ou la volonté de connaissance', 189-203.
   .6 Pasquier, Pierre, 'L'Armoire aux Masques ou la Poétique de RD', 205-84.
   .7 Giraud, Daniel, 'Astralités de Re-né', 285-97.

Bb513 Amadou, Robert, *Question de*, 45 (oct.-nov. 1981), 120-21. [CR Ab345]

Bb514 *Anon., Bulletin Critique du Livre Français*, 431 (nov. 1981), entry 116832, 1565. [CR Aa344]

Bb515 Henniger, Gerd, introduction to At347, 499-504. [Le GJ]

Bb516 *Anon., Bulletin Critique du Livre Français*, 432 (déc. 1981), entry 117135, 1727. [CR Ba488]

Bb517 R[omet], G[illes], *Magazine Littéraire*, 179 (déc. 1981), 12. [CR Ab345]

Bb518 Stéfan, Jude, *NRF*, LVIII, 347 (1 déc. 1981), 110-11. [CR Ba488]

*Bb519 Henniger, Gerd, 'Nein ist mein Name. RDs Orientalisierung des Geistes', *Protokolle* [Wein], 2 (1981). Repr. Bb557.

1982

Bb520 Reix, A., *Revue Philosophique de la France et de l'Etranger*,

CLXXII, 1 (jan.-mars 1982), 62. [CR Ab345]

Bb521 Couillard, Viviane, 'Aux frontières du surréalisme: Le GJ', *Mélusine (Cahiers du Centre de Recherches sur le Surréalisme)* [Lausanne], 3, no.'Marges non-frontières' (29 jan. 1981), 164-80.

Bb522 Tordeur, Jean, 'RD: la soif de l'être', *Le Soir* [Bruxelles], 44 (23 fév. 1982), 18. [CR Aa344, Ab345]

Bb523 Drachline, Pierre, 'Le Naufrage de RD', *Le Monde [des Livres]*, 11545 (12 mars 1982), 29. [CR Ab345]

Bb524 Texts in Aa356.
    .1 Virmaux, Alain & Virmaux, Odette, 'Poèmes retrouvés', 7-15. [RGL]
    .2 Virmaux, Alain & Virmaux, Odette, 'Poussière de diamants', 21-29. [RGL]

Bb525 Grössel, Hanns, 'RD und "Le GJ"', *Merkur* [Stuttgart], XXXVI, 5 (Mai 1982), 529-33. [CR At347]

Bb526 Waldberg, Michel, 'RD: la conquête du sommet', *Le Quotidien de Paris*, 769 (18 mai 1982), 21. [CR Aa344, Ab345]

Bb527 Martraix, Henri, *Europe*, 640-41 (août-sept. 1982), 225. [CR Aa356]

Bb528 Couillard, Viviane, 'La violence dans Le GJ', *Eidôlon (Cahiers du Laboratoire Pluridisciplinaire de Recherches sur L'Imagination Littéraire. Université de Bordeaux III)* [Bordeaux], 22, no.sp. 'Violence' (oct. 1982), 131-37.

Bb529 D.,G., 'Antonin Artaud et RGL ou le grand minuit des morts vivants', *Mot pour Mot* [Vitry], 7 (oct. 1982), 56-58. [CR Aa356]

Bb529a White, Kenneth, 'Le GJ' in *La figure du dehors. Essai* (Grasset, 1er trim. 1982, 238pp.), 140-48 (140-42). [RD]

Bb530 Posani, Giampiero, 'Le GJ', in *Letteratura francese. Le Correnti d'avanguardia* (Luciano Lucarini [Roma], 1982, vol.1, 328pp.), 267-305.

Bb531 Levi, Louise Landes, 'Introduction', in At355, 1-5. [RD]

The remaining entries for 1982 are reviews of 'Contre-ciel, plus', a reading of RD's poetry at the Théâtre des 400 coups (Paris) by

Secondary Material

Sylvain & Christiane Corthay, 15 sept.-15 oct. 1982:

Bb532 *Anon.*, 'Guillemets', *Le Figaro*, 11825 (10 sept. 1982), 25.

Bb533 *Anon.*, 'RD', *Les Echos. Le Quotidien de l'Economie*, 13719 (27 sept. 1982), 16.

Bb534 Madinier, Claire, 'RD aux 400 coups', *La Croix*, 30288 (30 sept. 1982), 17.

Bb535 Salino, Brigitte, *Les Nouvelles Litéraires*, 2855 (30 sept. 1982), 32.

Bb536 Surya, Michel, 'Contre-ciel plus', *Libération*, 433 (8 oct. 1982), 31.

Bb537 Gripari, Pierre, 'Chronique dramatique. Petits bourgeois et mégalomanes', *Ecrits de Paris*, 429 (nov. 1982), 115-121 120-21 on RD).

1983

Bb538 Couillard, Viviane, 'Une revue (presque surréaliste) des années 1928-1930: Le GJ', *Mélusine (Cahiers du Centre de Recherches sur le Surréalisme)* [Lausanne], 4, no.'Actes du colloque en Sorbonne, juin 1981: le livre surréaliste' (14 jan. 1983), 31-42.

Bb539 Cataño, José-Carlos, 'El absoluto, o si no cualquier cosa. RD hermano simplista', *Quimera* [Barcelona], 28 (febr. 1983), 16-21.

Bb540 Chénieux-Gendron, Jacqueline, same as Bb473 (L'Age d'Homme [Lausanne], 4 mars 1983, 388pp.).
Section on RD missing; refs to RD (13, 22, 26, 28, 58, 121, 171, 198, 200, 221, 299, 321, 334, 338).

Bb541 Lobet, Marcel, 'Deux témoins du retour à soi', *Revue Générale* [Bruxelles], 5 (mai 1983), 143-46. [CR Ab345]

*Bb542 Piot, Christine, 'Des circonstances d'un texte de RGL: *Monsieur Morphée empoisonneur public*', *Bulletin de liaison du Champ des Activités Surréalistes*, ERA 919, CNRS, 18 (juin 1983), 31-52.

Ba543 Powrie, Philip, 'Theory, structure and symbol in the work of RD', D.Phil.Thesis, University of Oxford (July 1983), v & 319pp.

Bb544 Lobet, Michel, 'RD et l'herméneutique littéraire', *A Rebours*, 25 (aut. 1983), 7-12.

Bb545 Picard, Michel, *Revue de l'Histoire littéraire de la France*, 5-6 (sept.-déc. 1983), 963-64. [CR Ab345]

Bb546 Couillard, Viviane, same as Bb475, new edition (Messidor/Editions Sociales, oct. 1983, 928pp.), 281-84. [Le GJ]

Bb547 *Anon.*, *Bulletin Critique du Livre Français*. 455 (nov. 1983), entry 124545, 1509-10. [CR Ab345]

1984

Bb548 Texts in *Actes. Les Cahiers d'Action Juridique*, 43-44, no.sp. 'Droit et Littérature' (mars 1984).
.1 Piot, Christine, 'RGL: un cas littéraire et juridique', 66-69.
.2 Dumas, Roland, 'Autour du cas RGL', 70.

Bb549 Catalogue of the 'Exposition RD' held at the Lycée Chanzy 16-21 Apr. 1984 and the Musée Rimbaud 25 Apr.-20 May 1984, both in Charleville-Mézières. Edited by Pascal Sigoda and Annie Bissarette (2e trim. 1984 [Charleville-Mézières], 42pp.).
Contains Bb433.1, extract from Ba199.6 and
.1 Sigoda, Pascal, 'RD et les Ardennes', 1-3, followed by short bio-bibliographical notes on pp.18, 22, 24, 29, 33-34.

Bb550 Pontiggia, Giuseppe, 'La "chiarezza" di [R]D' in *Il giardino delle Esperidi* (Adelphi [Milano], aprile 1984, 310pp.), 13-19. [CR At250)

Ba551 'Rimbaud, RD, Roger Vailland, RGL', no.sp. of *Rimbaldiana* (Editions du Musée-Bibliothèque Arthur Rimbaud [Charleville-Mézières], 2e trim. 1984, 48pp.).
Contains texts by RD (see Ab359) and RGL (see Ab362), and Bb463.

Bb552 Pinhas, L[uc], 'RD', in *Dictionnaire des littératures de langue française* (ed. J.-P. de Beaumarchais, Daniel Couty, Alain Rey; Bordas, mai 1984, [vol.1] A-F, xvi & 861pp.), 597-98.

Bb553 Marcaurelle, Roger, 'RD ou le somnicide perpétuel', *Liberté* [Montréal], XXVI, 3 (juin 1984), 147-54.

Bb554 Two texts in *Dictionnaire des littératures de langue française* (ed. J.-P. de Beaumarchais, Daniel Couty, Alain Rey; Bordas, sept. 1984, [vol.2] G-O, [vii] & 861-1684pp.).

.1 Vasseur, N[adine], 'RGL', 921-22.

.2 Vasseur, N[adine], 'Le GJ', 975.

Bb555 Vailland, Roger, same as Bb43 in *Chronique des années folles à la libération 1928/1945. Edition dirigée par René Ballet. Préface de Roland Leroy* (Messidor/Editions Sociales, déc. 1984, 508pp.), 61-62, 64-65. Also contains

.1 Ballet, René, 'La vie n'est qu'un jeu, Le GJ (1927-1929)' [commentary], 41-43 & 56-58.

Bb556 Scaiola, Anna Maria, 'RD', in *I Contemporanei. Letteratura francese* (Luciano Lucarini [Roma], ed. Massimo Colesanti & Luigi de Nardis, 1984, 784pp.), 323-35. In section 'Surrealismo e Dintorni'.

Bb557 Henniger, Gerd, same as Bb519 in *Spuren in Offene. Essays über Literatur* (Carl Hanser Verlag [München-Wien], 1984, 249pp.), 142-88. [RD]

1985

Bb558 Couillard, Viviane, '*Le GJ*/groupe/rupture' in Anne Roche & Christian Tarting (eds), *Des années trente: groupes et ruptures. Actes du colloque organisé par l'antenne de l'U.R.L. no.5 à l'Université de Provence I, 5-7 mai 1983* (Coll. 'Les publications de l'U.R.L. no.5: Lexicologie et Terminologie Littéraires Contemporaines', no.7, Centre National de la Recherche Scientifique, jan. 1985, 300pp.), [237]-46.

Ba559 Dumas, Roland, *Plaidoyer pour RGL. Avec la collaboration de Christine Piot suivi de Le Cristal dans l'éclair par Serge Sautreau* (Gallimard, nrf, 10 mai 1985, 256pp.).
Contains Bb1, Bb8, Bb12, Bb21, Bb36, Bb168, Bb196, Bb198.2, Bb234, Bb437.2, Bb437.3, the full version of Bb283.1 and Ba488.7 and the following letters:

.1 Firmat, Mme, to Pierre Minet dated 3 jan. 1944, 101-02.

.2 Pierre-Quint, Léon, to Pierre Minet dated 3 fév. 1944 (extract), 102.

.3 Lecomte, Edmond, to Arthur Adamov dated 29 oct. 1947, 103-04.

.4 Urbain, Blanche, to Robert Gallimard dated 30 mars 1953, 105. Also appears on pp.219-20.

.5 Urbain, Blanche, to Pierre Minet dated 23 juin 1961, 108.

.6 Bazin, Hervé, to Roland Dumas dated 2 déc. 1962, 109.

.7   Mauriac, François, to Roland Dumas dated 18 déc. 1962, 109.
.8   Picon, Gaëtan, to Blanche Urbain dated 1 fév. 1965, 112-13.
.9   Urbain, Blanche, to Gaëtan Picon dated 8 fév. 1965, 113.
.10 Lecomte, Edmond, to RGL dated 20 sept. 1927, 205.
.11 Lecomte, Edmond, to RGL dated 12 avr. 1941, 205-06.
.12 Lecomte, Edmond, to RGL dated 12 août 1942, 206.
.13 Lecomte, Edmond, to RGL dated 13 août 1942, 206-07.
.14 Lecomte, Edmond, to Mme Firmat dated 16 jan. 1944, 207-08.
.15 Lecomte, Edmond, to Mme Firmat dated 25 jan. 1944, 208-09.
.16 Lecomte, Edmond, to Mme Firmat dated 4 fév. 1944, 209.
.17 Lecomte, Edmond, to Arthur Adamov dated 12 fév. 1944, 210-11.
.18 Laire, Mathilde, to RGL dated [1925-1926?], 212.
.19 Robertfrance, Jacques, to RGL dated 1 août 1927, 213.
.20 Firmat, Mme, to Edmond Lecomte dated 13 mars 1944, 216-17.
.21 Laire, Paul, to Mme Firmat dated 26 jan. 1944, 217-18.
.22 Laire, Paul, to Pierre Minet dated fév. 1959, 218-19.
.23 Gallimard, Robert, to Blanche Urbain dated 29 mai 1953, 220.
.24 Urbain, Blanche, to Robert Gallimard dated 16 juin 1953, 220-21.
.25 Gallimard, Robert, to Blanche Urbain dated 6 août 1953, 221.
.26 Daumal, Véra, to Pierre Minet dated 4 déc. 1958, 221-22.
.27 Minet, Pierre, to Blanche Urbain dated 19 juin 1961, 222.
.28 Bombaron, Georges, to Pierre Minet dated 8 mai 1967, 223.
.29 Cassou, Jean, to Pierre Minet dated 2 nov. 1968 (extract), 224.
.30 Latarget, René, [to Bernard Faupin?] dated 28 nov. 1966, 225.
.31 Pontinet, A., to Bernard Faupin dated 29 déc. 1966, 225-26.
.32 Lallemand, G., to Bernard Faupin dated 4 fév. 1967, 226-27.
There are also the following 'déclarations de soutien à l'Association des Amis de RGL':
.33 Caillois, Roger, 114.
.34 Cassou, Jean, 115.
.35 Paulhan, Jean, 115.
.36 Suarès, Carlo, 223.
.37 Aron, Raymond, 224.
.38 Bastide, François-Régis, 224.
.39 Amadou, Robert, 224.
.40 Lambroso, Fernand, 224.

Bb560 Texts in *Le Monde [des Livres]*, 12545 (31 mai 1985).
   .1   Dumas, Roland, 'RGL et Roland Dumas' [interview with Raphaël Sorin], 26.
   .2   *Anon.*, '"Le GJ est irrémédiable"', 26.
   .3   Sorin, Raphaël, 'Entrée des fantômes', 26. [CR Aa365]
   .4   Sorin, Raphaël, 'Artür Harfaux, le dernier témoin', 26. [CR Bb568]
   .5   Sorin, Raphaël, 'La ferveur de Mme H.J.Maxwell', 26. [RGL]

Bb561 Brochier, Jean-Jacques, 'Les règles de l'héritage', *Magazine Littéraire*, 221 (juill.-août 1985), 8-9. [CR Ba559]

Bb562 Knapp, Bettina, 'RD et le *Natya-Castra [sic]: un Coniunctio oppositorum'*, *Le Siècle Eclaté. 3: Le Texte et son double* (Revue des Lettres Modernes/L'Icosathèque (20th)), 8 (juill. 1985), 125-37.

Bb563 Virmaux, Odette, & Virmaux, Alain, 'Correspondance: A propos du GJ', *Le Monde [des Livres]*, 12581 (12 juillet 1985), 14. [CR Bb560]

Bb564 Boisdeffre, Pierre de, same as Bb134, new edition in two vols under title *Histoire de la littérature de langue française des années 1930 aux années 1980*. The substantial material on RD is contained in the section 'Au-delà des apparences' with the subtitle 'L'Aventure de RD', in vol.1 *Roman, Théâtre. Nouvelle édition entièrement refondue* (Librairie Académique Perrin, 10 juill. 1985, 1390pp.), 1020-21; the bio-bibliography is contained in vol.2 *Poésie. Idées. Dictionnaire des Auteurs* (24 sept. 1985, 1260pp.), 902.
This vol. also contains a bio-bibliography of RGL on 967.

Bb565 Duverger, Maurice, 'La parole du poète baillonné, *Lu*, 16 (sept. 1985), 49. [CR Ba559]

Bb566 Two texts in *Europe*, LXIII, 679-80 (nov.-déc. 1985).
   .1   Miguel, André, 'Le Grand Jeu du Non', 147-54. [RD, RGL]
   .2   Miguel, André, 194-95. [CR Ba559]

Bb567 Texts in Aa367. Contains Bb182 and
   .1   Sautreau, Serge, 'Avant lettre', 7-10.

*Bb568 Harfaux, Artür, *Demain il sera trop tard* (Le Nyctalope [Amiens], 1985). [Le GJ]

1986

Bb569 D[urozoi], G[érard], 'Le GJ', *Magazine Littéraire*, 226 (jan. 1986), 11. [CR Aa367]

Bb570 Virmaux, A[lain], et O[dette], *La Quinzaine Littéraire*, 456 (1 fév. 1986), 4. [CR Ba559]

Bb571 Barry-Couillard, Viviane, 'La ville onirique de RD', *Eidôlon (Cahiers du Laboratoire Pluridisciplinaire de Recherches sur l'Imagination Littéraire. Université de Bordeaux III)* [Bordeaux], 27, no.sp. 'L'Imaginaire de la ville' (fév. 1986), 185-208.

Bb572 Paulhan, Jean, *Choix de lettres. Par Dominique Aury et Jean-Claude Zylberstein. Revu et annoté par Bernard Leuilliot. I. 1917-1936. La littérature est une fête* (Gallimard, nrf, 5 fév. 1986, 510pp.). Contains the following letters:
    .1 To Marcel Arland dated [nov. 1930], 199-202. [GJ]
    .2 To RD dated [30 nov. 1930], 202-03.
    .3 To RD dated [nov. 1930], 203.
    .4 To André Rolland de Renéville dated 8 déc. 1931, 216-19. [GJ]
    .5 To RD dated [mai 1932], 245-46.
    .6 To RD dated [mai 1932], 246.
    .7 To André Rolland de Renéville dated 28 juin 1932, 255-57. [RD]
    .8 To André Rolland de Renéville dated 28 [nov. 1932], 276-78. [RD]
    .9 To Léon Bopp dated 27 août 1934, 324. [RD]
    .10 To Franz Hellens dated [mai 1935], 341-42. [RD]
    .11 To RD dated [30 oct. 1935], 354-55.
    .12 To RD dated 3 [oct. 1936], 414-15.

Bb573 Stéfan, Jude, *NRF*, 398 (1 mars 1986), 89-91. [CR Aa367]

Bb574 Texts in Jean Paulhan & Francis Ponge, *Correspondance 1923-1968. Edition critique annotée par Claire Boaretto. Vol.I, 1923-1946* (Gallimard, nrf, 18 juin 1986, 372pp.). Contains the following letters:
    .1 Paulhan to Ponge dated 6 nov. 1932, no.139, 148. [RD]
    .2 Paulhan to Ponge dated [début jan. 1933], no.145, 153. [RD, RGL]
    .3 Ponge to Paulhan dated 24 jan. 1935, no.182, 184. [RD]
    .4 Paulhan to Ponge dated 6 jan. 1939, no.227, 229. [RD]

Bb575   Couillard-Barry, Viviane, 'Révélation/Révolution ou le
         Casse-Dogme du GJ', *Dada-Surrealismo: Precursores, Marginales
         y Heterodoxes. Actes du Colloque de Cádiz, 19-22 Novembre 1985*
         ([Cadiz] Servicio de Publicaciones Universidad de Cádiz, 1986,
         203pp.), 26-28.

Bb576   Texts in At369. Contains translations of Bb47.2, Bb152.1 and
         .1   Shattuck, Roger, 'Translator's Note', 7-8. This also contains
         a translation of Bb494. There is also a biographical note
         (1) and a bibliography (25-26).

                                1987

Bb577   Schwartz, Leonard, 'The Forgotten as Contemporary. Benjamin
         Fondane and RGL', *Literary Review* [Madison, New Jersey], XXX,
         3, no.sp. 'New Writing in French' (Spring 1987), 465-67.

Bb578   Miguel, André, 'La pensée contemporaine de RGL', *Europe*,
         LXIV, 698-99 (juin-juill. 1987), 170-77.

*Bb579 Two texts in *Courrier du Centre International d'Etudes
         Poétiques*, 175 (sept.-oct. 1987).
         .1   Alexandre, Didier, 'Frontières de RD', 21-33.
         .2   Miguel, André, 'Révolte, négation et abnégation chez RD',
         35-45.

Bb580   Shattuck, Roger, 'Translator's note' in At371, 59-63.

                                1988

Bb581   Powrie, Phil, 'Automatic Writing: Breton, Daumal, Hegel',
         French Studies [Oxford], XLII, 2 (April 1988), 177-93.

INDEXES

Index of Aa Works by René Daumal

Index of Ab + Ac Works by René Daumal

Index of Ab + Ac Works by René Daumal

'A propos d'Uday Shankar et de quelques
autres Hindous', Ab49, At54, Aa184,
Aa265.1, Aa288, At355
'A propos d'un jugement inédit de Victor
Cousin sur Giordano Bruno', Ab33.4,
Ab254, Aa288, Ab308
'L'Art hindou', Ab109, Ab345.8
'L'Asphyxie et l'expérience de l'absurde',
Ab254.3, Ab269, Aa288, Ab308, At347
'Au cœur de la nuit brille l'anti-lueur...',
Aa193.38, Ab202
'Au Musée des Colonies', Ab63.1
'Au Musée d'Ethnographie du Trocadéro
[L'époque héroïque...]', Ab57.5
'Au Musée d'Ethnographie du Trocadéro
[On ne peut quand même pas...]',
Ab65.2
'A une ancienne (ah 'la la [sic]) compagne',
Ab323
'L'Autre Abandon', Aa193.15, Aa271,
At295
'Avant-propos', Ac5, At32, At239, Ab242,
Ab254, Ab269, Ac297, Ab308, At309,
Ab324, Ab335, At347
'Les Ballets Joos', Ab64
'Le Bouddhisme, ses doctrines et ses
méthodes, par Alexandra David-Neel',
Ab96.1, Aa287, At355
'Le Bourreau du Pérou, par G. Ribemont-
Dessaignes, Ab7
'Brève révélation sur la mort et le chaos',
Aa99.13, Aa193, Aa271
'Les Broderies de Marie Monnier', Ab89
'Bubu-Magazine (numéro spécimen &
numéro deux)', Ab203
'Casse-cœur', Ab30.2, Ab187, Aa193,
Aa271
'Le Casse-dogme', Ab335.1
'Le Catéchisme', Aa186, Ab247, Aa248,
At251, Aa287
'La Cavalcade', Ab29.3, Aa193, Aa271
'Cave des cœurs...', Ab191.3, Aa193

'Les Cenci d'Antonin Artaud et Autour
d'une mère de J.-L. Barrault', Ab88,
Ab338
'C'est le propre de la pensée méta-
physique...', Ab345.11
'La Chair de terreur', Aa193.8
'Chanson réaliste', Aa193.35, Ab253
'Chez Victor Hugo. Les Tables Tournantes
de Jersey, par Gustave Simon',
Ab14.8, Ab254, Aa288, Ab308
'Chronique médicale', Aa208.2
'La Chute', Ab28, Aa193, Aa271
'Civilisation', Ab29.2, Aa99, Aa193,
At239, Aa271
'Clavicules d'un grand jeu poétique', Ab44,
Aa99.1, Aa193, At220a, Aa271, Aa288
Collective declaration on Roger Vailland's
withdrawal from Le GJ, Ac34.1,
Ab254, Ab308, Ab363
'Comme dit la chanson', Ab86, Aa193
(see also Aa116 and reprints)
'Comment tout recommence', Aa99.14,
Aa193, Aa271
'Le Comte de Lautréamont et la critique',
Ab35, Ab277, Aa288
'Le Comte de Lautréamont et la justice
tchécoslovaque', Ac31, Ac34, Ab269,
Ac297, Ab308
'La Consolatrice', Aa193.14, Aa271
'Creux de songe', Aa193.21, Aa271
'La Critique des critiques', Ac15.3,
Ab254, Ac297, Ab308
'Cruautés', Ab187.2, Aa193
'Danse sacrée', Ab72.2
'Les Déceptions', Ab185.6, Aa193
'Défi', Aa193.28, Aa271
'De l'attitude critique devant la Poésie',
Ab18, Aa184, Aa288, Ab359
'De quelques sculptures de sauvages',
Ab16, At239, Aa288
'La Dernière Race', Aa193.26, Aa271

145

René Daumal and Roger Gilbert-Lecomte

Index of Ae Works by René Daumal

Death in the afternoon, Ernest Hemingway
Ae108, Ae173, Ae179, Ae216, Ae228,
Ae231, Ae236, Ae289
Essays on Zen Buddhism, D.T. Suzuki,
Ae138.1, Ae138.2, Ae138.3, Ae143,
Ae153, Ae154, Ae157, Ae158, Ae165,

Ae190, Ae206, Ae285, Ae286, Ab345
The Kena Upanishad, Shrî Aurobindo,
Ae156, Ae174, Ae199, Ae279
Murder in black, F.D. Grierson, Ae103
My Selves, N. Lucas & E. Graham,
Ae117

Index of As Works by René Daumal

Bhagavad-Gita, As188.1, Aa265, Aa271
Bhartrihari, As136.6, As266.4, Aa271,
At284, As303.6, Ab345, At355
Bodhicaryâvatâra, As303.1, As303.5
Brihadâranyaka Upanishad, As128, Aa265,
Aa271, At284, At355
Chândogya Upanishad, As243.2, Aa265,
As303.2
Fragments (unidentified), As215.1, Ab240,
Ab294, As303.7
Mânavadharmaçastra, As188.2, As243.1,
Aa265, As303.3
Mohamadgara, As312
Nâtya-çâstra, As92, As136.2, As136.4,
As212, At251, Aa265, Aa271, At284,
At355

Pantcha Tantra, As266.2, At284, As303.4
Rasataranginî, As136.5, Aa271, At284,
At355
Rig-Veda, As227, As241, As243.3, Aa265,
As266.1, Aa271, Ab294, Ab345,
As346.1, As346.2, As346.3, As346.4,
At355
Sâhitya-darpana, As85, As136.1, As136.3,
As136.7, At251, Aa265, Aa271, At284,
At355
Shukla Yajur Vêda, As215.4
Shvetashvatara Upanishad, As215.2
Taittirîya Upanishad, As215.3
Viçanatha Kaviraja, As266.3

Index of At Works by René Daumal

'A propos d'Uday Shankar et de quelques
autres Hindous', At54
'Clavicules d'un grand jeu poétique',
At220a
[Collection] *Akzente*, At347
[Collection] *Almanacco dello Specchio*,
At295
[Collection] *La Conoscenza di Sè.
Scritti et lettere 1939-1941*,
At284
[Collection] *Il "Grand Jeu". Scritti
di RGL e RD*, At239
[Collection] *I Poteri della Parola*, At251

[Collection] *Rasa, or, Knowledge of the
Self. Essays on Indian Aesthetics
and Selected Sanskrit Studies*, At355
[Collection] *ReD*, At32
'Entre deux chaises', At325
'L'Envers du décor', At93
La Grande Beuverie, At272, At332,
At333, At349, At364
Letter to Christoflour, Raymond, dated
2 giugnio 1940 (extracts), At284.13
1 aprile 1941 (extract), At284.18
Letter to Daumal, Jack, dated [settembre
1940] (extract), At284.14

Index of Ab + Ac Works by Roger Gilbert-Lecomte

Index of Aa Works by Roger Gilbert-Lecomte

Index of Ab + Ac Works by Roger Gilbert-Lecomte

'A forme et se saisit...', Aa280.82,
Aa319

'Agir', Aa315.1, Aa319

'L'Aile d'endormir', Aa61.29, At245,
Aa319

'A la chance fragile...', Aa205.7,
Aa301

'L'Alchimie de l'œil; le cinéma, forme
de l'esprit', Ab59, Aa301

'Amour, amour!', Aa211.3, Aa319

'Angoisses', Aa315.4

'Anti-soleil', Aa356.1

'A perpétuité', Aa319.97

'Appel à la lutte', Ac79, Ac80,
Ac170, Ac340

'Après Rimbaud la mort des Arts', Ab22.1,
At245, Ab256, Ab275, Aa283, Aa301,
At305, Ab317, Ab362

'Après sa mort...', Aa301.10

'L'arbre dans l'homme...', Ab168.3,
Aa205, Aa296, Aa301

'*L'Arbre de visages*, par Marcel
Jouhandeau', Ab134, Aa205.26,
Aa301.38, Aa356

'Les Arguties de la conscience du rêve.
La paralysie des côtes, l'engourdis-
sement des membres', Ab196.3, Aa205,
At318, Aa319

'Arsenal', Ab196.1, Aa205, Aa319

'L'Art de la danse', Aa61.17, Aa319

'Les Atalantes', Aa319.67

'L'Atout du noir', Aa319.23

'L'aube - Chante l'alouette...', Aa319.24

'Au sortir du cellier...', Aa315.9,
Aa319

'Autant que le cœur solaire...', Aa319.58

'Autobus...', Aa319.84

'Au vent du nord', Aa205.3, Aa319

'Avant-propos', Ab11, At38, At245,
Ab246, Ab256, Ab275, Aa301,
Ab317, At318, Ab328, Ab339,
At352

'Bénarès violet au Kiel [*sic*] viride',
Aa319.74

'La Bonne Vie', Aa61.2, Aa205, At318,
Aa319

'Bouquet sur ma tombe', Aa319.30

'BoXe Match [*sic*], Aa315.7, Aa319

'La branche des marronniers...', Ab2.1,
Aa316, Aa319

'Brouillard sur la mer', Ab2.8, Aa316,
Aa319

'Le bruit des oiseaux...', Ab171.10,
Aa301

'Bulles', Aa319.73

'La cage du thorax...', Ab168.4, Aa205,
Aa296, Aa301

'Cantilène des soleils morts', Aa319.60

'Carnet de route d'un trépassé', Aa205.10,
Aa315, Aa319

'Catastrophes...', Aa319.93

'La Cathartique du néant. La sublimation
de l'Antéros', Aa301.14

'La cathédrale dans les brumes...', Ab2.9,
Aa316, Aa319

'Cave en plein ciel', Aa319.86

'Celle qui fut Héloïse...', Aa319.19

'Ce n'est rien...', Ab168.1, Aa205,
Aa301

'Ce que devrait être la peinture, ce que
sera Sima', Ab24, At27, Ab225,
At245, Ab255, Ab275, Aa301, Ab339

'Ce que voit et ce que fait voir Sima
aujourd'hui', Ab36, Aa301

'Ce soir le soleil...', Aa319.35

'Ce vieillard ridicule...', Aa319.18

'La Chanson du prisonnier', Aa104.5,
Aa205, Aa319

'Chanson française', Aa61.11, Aa205,
Aa319

'Chant de mort Cristal d'ouragan',
Aa104.1, Aa319

'Le Chant malin du rat', Aa61.7,
Aa319

3 jan. 1927, Aa280.55
17 fév. 1927, Ab209.2, Aa280
13 oct. 1927, Aa280.59
[1927], Aa280.60, Aa280.63,
    Aa280.64, Aa280.65
23 mai 1928, Aa280.75
[1928], Aa280.69, Aa280.70,
    Aa280.71, Aa280.72, Aa280.73,
    Aa280.74 Aa280.77
[1929], Aa280.78
18 fév. 1930, Aa280.79
23 avr. 1930, Aa280.80
28 avr. 1930, Aa280.83
17 fév. 1931 (extract), Ab273.5,
    Aa280
[1931], Aa280.84, Aa280.85
16 mars 1932, Aa280.86
24 mars 1932, Aa280.88
mars 1932 (extract), Ab273.6, Aa280
28 juin 1932, Ab273.8, Aa280
2 août 1932, Aa280.90
11 août 1932, Aa280.93
13 août 1932, Aa280.94
17 nov. 1932, Aa280.96
1932, Aa280.91, Aa280.92
[1932], Ab264.1, Aa280, Aa280.98,
    Aa280.99, Aa280.100, Aa280.101,
    Aa280.102
22 jan. 1933, Aa280.103
undated, Aa280.28
Letters to Rolland de Renéville, André,
    dated [1928], Ab357.1
16 mars 1928, Ab357.2
21 juill. 1928, Ab282, Ab366
13 juill. 1929 (telegram), Ac274,
    Ab275
7 nov. 1929, Ab273.3
undated, Ab304
Letter to Sernet, Claude, undated, Aa237.1,
    Ab350

Letters to Sima, Joseph, dated 5 oct.
    1933, Aa319.95
    undated (FMS), Aa319.94
Letter to Tagore, Rabindranath, dated
    26 juin 1930, Ac217, Ab264, Ab275
Letters to Vailland, Roger, and RD dated
    oct. 1925, Aa280.24
    5 nov. 1925, Aa280.25
    [1925], Aa280.33
    13 fév. 1926, Aa280.37
    13 mars 1926, Ab275.2, Aa280
    19 mai 1926, Aa280.38
    2 juin 1926, Aa280.39
    13 juin 1926, Aa280.40
    5 juill. 1926, Aa280.41
    6 oct. 1926, Aa280.45
    14 nov. 1926, Aa280.49
    26 nov. 1926, Aa280.50
    [1926], Aa280.52, Aa280.54
    [1927], Aa280.61, Aa280.62,
        Aa280.66, Aa280.67
    [1928], Aa280.68
Letters to Vailland, Roger, dated sept.
    1924, Ab263.3, Aa280
    25 avr. 2925 [*sic*], Aa280.16
    mai 1925 (extracts), Ab275.1, Aa280
    10 [août 1925], Aa280.18
    12 août 1925, Aa280.19, Ab366
    2 sept. 1925, Aa280.21, Ab366
    2 oct. 1925, Aa280.22
    11 nov. 1925, Aa280.26
    13 déc. 1925, Aa280.27
    [1925], Aa280.31, Aa280.32
    3 jan. 1926 (extract), Ab273.1,
        Ab275, Aa280
    24 jan. 1926 (extract), Ab273.2,
        Aa280
    6 juill. 1926, Aa280.42
    21 août 1926, Aa280.43
    8 sept. 1926, Aa280.44
    1926 (extract), Ab275.3, Aa280

Index of At Works by Roger Gilbert-Lecomte

Selective Index of Proper Names

Selective Index of Proper Names

Index of Authors for Secondary Material Articles

Index of Authors for Secondary Material Books, Theses and Special Numbers

Achirian, Josiane, Ba287

Agasse, Jean-Michel, Ba331

Biès, Jean, Ba184, Ba204, Ba376

Cettour, Françoise, Ba336

[Collection] *Cahiers de l'Herne*, Ba239

[Collection] *Cahiers de la Maison de la Culture André Malraux*, Ba464

[Collection] *CdS,* Ba73

[Collection] *Hermès*, Ba202

[Collection] *L'Originel* [Le GJ], Ba465

[Collection] *L'Originel* [RD], Ba512

[Collection] *La Grive*, Ba199

[Collection] *Rimbaldiana*, Ba551

Dumas, Roland, Ba559

Feuillette, Christian-Paul, Ba262

Guichard, Gérard, Ba481

Jacques, Chantal, Ba477

Knight, Kelton Wallace, Ba398

Lepage, Jacques, Ba347

Melrose, Robin, Ba263

Néaumet, Jean, Ba410

Powrie, Philip, Ba543

Random, Michel, Ba283

Virmaux, Alain & Virmaux, Odette, Ba488

Index of Authors for Secondary Material Articles

Abastado, Claude, Bb343, Bb405

Abellio, Raymond, Bb365

Accarias, Jean-Louis, Bb439, Ba465.6, Ba512.2

Adamov, Arthur, Bb34, Bb35, Bb36, Bb46, Bb75, Bb101.1, Bb234, Bb260, Bb437.2, Ba559

Aga-Rossi, Laura, Bb458

Agasse, Jean-Michel, Ba465.8, Ba465.9, Ba512.3

Alexandrian, Sarane, Bb389

Amadou, Robert, Bb513, Ba559.39

Amette, Jacques-Pierre, Bb490

Angenot, Marc, Bb276, Bb354

Anon., Bb3, Bb37.2, Ba73.4, Bb137, Bb147, Bb196, Ba199.7, Ba202.1, Bb208, Bb214, Bb217.5, Ba239.5, Bb247, Bb251.2, Bb256, Bb299, Bb303, Bb305, Bb306, Bb308, Bb311, Bb317, Bb321, Bb324, Bb330, Bb358, Bb359, Bb391, Bb396, Bb426.2, Bb435, Bb443, Bb445.1, Bb445.2, Ba465.14, Bb468, Bb492, Bb514, Bb516, Bb532, Bb533, Bb547, Ba559, Bb560.2

Aragon, Louis, Bb198.2, Ba488, Ba559

Aragon, Louis, & Breton, André, Bb9, Bb45, Ba283, Bb485

Aribaut, Robert, Bb312

Aron, Raymond, Ba559.37

Artaud, Antonin, Bb21, Bb160, Bb160.1, Bb374, Ba488, Ba559

Attal, Jean-Pierre, Bb222, Bb265

Audejean, Christian, Bb258, Bb448

Ayguesparse, Albert, Bb223

Ballerini, Michel, Bb368

Ballet, René, Bb555.1

Baron, Jacques, Bb286

Barry-Couillard, Viviane, *see Couillard, Viviane*

Bars, Henry, Bb278

Bastide, François-Régis, Ba559.38

Bazan, Paul, Bb364.2

Bazin, Hervé, Ba559.6

Béarn, Pierre, Bb449

Begot, Jean-Pierre, Bb390

Benoist, Luc, Bb372, Bb379

Berchan, Richard, Bb361

Bernard, Michel, Bb266

Index of Authors for Secondary Material Articles

Lambert, Jean-Clarence, Ba464.11

Lambilliotte, Maurice, Bb207

Lambroso, Fernand, Ba559.40

Lams, Mariane, Ba465.3

Landon, Rosemary, Bb261

Lapouge, Gilles, Bb171

Larcher, Hubert, Bb29, Ba512

Latarget, René, Ba559.30

Laude, André, Bb425

Lazarus, Maria, Bb126

Lebedev, Jorge, Bb160b

Lebois, André, Bb128

Leclec'h, Guy, Bb69, Bb252

Lecomte, Edmond, Ba283.1, Ba559, Ba559.3, Ba559.10, Ba559.11, Ba559.12, Ba559.13, Ba559.14, Ba559.15, Ba559.16, Ba559.17

Lecomte, Marcel, Bb118, Bb131, Bb141, Bb144

Lecrique, Camille, Bb92, Ba199.10

Legris, Jacques, Ba488.6

Leheutre, Claude, Bb466

Lehner, Frederick, Bb78

Le Marchand, Jean, Bb307

Lepage, Jacques, Bb150, Bb158, Bb159, Bb166, Ba199.4, Ba464.5

Lestrient, Eric, Bb434

Leuwers, Daniel, Bb459, Bb469

Levi, Louise Landes, Bb531

Lévy, Tony, Bb421

Linhartová, Věra, Bb385, Bb482, Ba488

Lobet, Marcel, Bb49, Bb215, Bb541, Bb544

Loiseau, Martin, Bb290

Loranquin, Albert, Bb87, Bb108

Madinier, Claire, Bb534

Magny, Olivier de, Bb88, Bb110

Maillet, Christian, Bb294

Mambrino, Jean, Bb499

Marcaurelle, Roger, Bb553

Marion, Denis, Bb59

Mars, Paul-Claude, Bb62

Martraix, Henri, Bb527

Masui, Jacques, Ba73.5, Bb175, Ba202.4, Bb226.2, Ba239.3, Bb248, Bb273, Bb362

Mathias, Pierre, Bb100, Bb153

Matthews, J.H., Bb221

Maublanc, René, Bb1, Bb428, Ba488, Ba559

Mauriac, Claude, Bb83, Bb104, Bb230, Bb257, Bb289, Bb329, Bb355, Bb380, Bb433.1, Bb549

Mauriac, François, Ba559.7

Mavel, Gérard, Ba199.13

Maxwell, H. Josèphe, Bb426.1, Bb427, Bb455, Ba464.1, Ba465.2, Bb480, Ba488, Ba512.1, Ba512.4

Maxwell, H. Josèphe, & Rugafiori, Claudio, Bb494, Bb576

Méautis, Georges, Bb54, Bb140

Merlin, Irène, Bb393

Mertens, Pierre, Bb367

Michaud, Marcel, Bb103

Miguel, André, Bb318, Bb395, Ba464.3, Bb566.1, Bb566.2, Bb578, Bb579.2

Minet, Pierre, Bb30.1, Bb40, Bb71.1, Bb101.2, Bb130, Bb173, Ba199.5, Ba202.7, Ba239.2, Bb267.1, Bb268, Bb320, Bb332, Bb364.1, Bb369, Bb378.1, Bb429.1, Bb437.1, Ba488, Ba559.27

Minet, Pierre, & Random, Michel, Bb292

Minet, Pierre, & Sorin, Raphaël, Bb253

Morvan, J.-B., Bb236

Morvan, J.-J., Bb106

Mottaz, Philippe, Bb447

N., Ch., Bb397

Nadeau , Maurice, Bb32, Bb133, Bb177, Bb187, Bb232, Bb246, Bb272

Navarri, Roger, Bb479

Naville, Pierre, Bb420

Néaumet, Jean, Bb427, Ba512.5

Needham, Jacob, Bb386.1

Index of Authors for Secondary Material Articles

Nelli, René, Bb400a

Nelson, Hilda, Bb370, Bb470

Neveux, Georges, Ba488.5

Nimier, Roger, Bb60, Bb64, Bb176, Bb183

Noël, Bernard, Bb339, Bb344, Bb392, Ba488

Norton, David, Bb154

Noulet, Emilie, Bb38, Bb181

O., A., Bb423.1

Oster, Daniel, Bb388

Oster, Pierre, Bb111

Pache, Jean, Bb442

Parisse, Jacques, Bb338

Pasquier, Pierre, Bb418, Bb478, Ba512.6

Paulhan, Jean, Bb72, Bb217.4, Bb423, Ba488, Ba559.35, Bb572.1, Bb572.2, Bb572.3, Bb572.4, Bb572.5, Bb572.6, Bb572.7, Bb572.8, Bb572.9, Bb572.10, Bb572.11, Bb572.12, Bb574.1, Bb574.2, Bb574.4

Pauwels, Louis, Bb48, Bb71, Bb254

Péju, Pierre, Bb430

Pellegrini, Aldo, Bb160a, Bb508a

Pellus, Daniel, Bb245

Périn, Luc, Ba199.6, Bb549

Perniola, Mario, Bb259

Perrier, Jean-Claude, Bb511

Perros, Georges, Bb67, Bb507

Petifaux, Georges, Bb57

Peyrot, Françoise, Bb298

Pia, Pascal, Bb300, Bb350

Picard, Michel, Bb411, Bb545

Picon, Gaëtan, Bb156, Bb242, Bb412, Bb413, Ba559.8

Pierre-Quint, Léon, Bb8, Bb12, Bb18, Bb30.2, Bb201, Ba283, Bb428, Ba488, Ba559, Ba559.2

Pignarre, R., Bb314, Bb340

Pinhas, Luc, Bb552

Piot, Christine, Bb542, Bb548.1

Plazy, G., Bb212

Pleynet, Marcelin, Bb178

Ponge, Francis, Bb574.3

Pontiggia, Giuseppe, Bb550

Pontinet, A., Ba559.31

Posani, Giampiero, Bb530

Poulliart, Raymond, Bb346, Bb400, Bb409

Powrie, Phil, Bb581

Puyaubert, Jean, Ba488.3

Rainord, Manuel, Ba73.1

Random, Michel, Bb191, Bb197, Bb198.1, Ba199.8, Ba202.2, Bb209, Bb210, Bb284, Ba465.7, Ba488

Rappo, Pierre, Bb491

Raymond, Marcel, Bb27, Bb42

Recanati, Jean, Bb243.1, Bb316, Ba488

Reich, Zdenko, Ba488.2

Reix, A., Bb520

Revel, Jean-François, Bb233, Bb237

Ribemont-Dessaignes, Georges, Bb135, Ba199.2, Bb371, Ba465.4, Ba465.12, Ba488

Rich, Auguste, & Gaudin, Louis, Bb436

Richaud, André, Bb474

Richer, Jean, Ba202.5

Robert, Francis, Bb2

Robert, Marthe, & Adamov, Arthur, Bb46, Bb101

Robertfrance, Jacques, Ba559.19

Rode, Henri, Bb94

Rolland de Renéville, André, Bb23, Bb25, Bb31, Bb33.1, Bb47.1, Bb71.2, Ba488

Romet, Gilles, Bb517

Roudaut, Jean, Bb148, Bb185, Ba202.6, Bb348, Ba464.2

Rougemont, Denis de, Bb22

Rousseaux, André, Bb50, Bb58, Bb76, Bb77, Bb85, Bb93, Bb105, Bb139

Rousselot, Jean, Bb84, Bb301, Bb326, Bb327

Roy, Bruno, Bb167

RESEARCH BIBLIOGRAPHIES & CHECKLISTS
Edited by
A.D. Deyermond, J.R. Little and J.E. Varey

25. Geoghegan, C.   Louis Aragon: essai de bibliographie
                         I. Œuvres, 2 vols, 1979
                         II. Critique, *in preparation*

26. Lowe, D.K.   Benjamin Constant: an annotated bibliography of critical editions and studies (1946-1978), 1979

27. Mason, B.   Michel Butor: a checklist, 1979

28. Shirt, D.J.   The Old French Tristan poems: a bibligraphical guide, 1980

29. McGaha, M.D.   The Theatre in Madrid during the Second Republic: a checklist, 1979

30. Stathatos, C.C.   A Gil Vicente bibliography (1940-1975), 1980

31. Bleikasten, A.   Arp: bibliographie
                         I. Écrits/Dichtung, 1981
                         II. Critique/Kritik, 1983

32. Bergman, H.E. and S.E. Szmuk   A Catalogue of *Comedias sueltas* in the New York Public Library, 2 vols, 1980-81

33. Best, M.   Ramón Pérez de Ayala: an annotated bibliography of criticism, 1980

34. Clive, H.P.   Marguerite de Navarre: an annotated bibliography, 1982

35. Sargent-Baur, B.N. and R.F. Cook   *Aucassin et Nicolete*: a critical bibliography, 1981

36. Nelson, B.   Émile Zola: a selective analytical bibliography, 1982

37. Field, T.   Maurice Barrès: a selective critical bibliography, 1948-79, 198

38. Bell, S.M.   Nathalie Sarraute: a bibliography, 1982

39. Kinder, A.G.   Spanish Protestants and Reformers in the sixteenth century: bibliography, 1983

40. Clive, H.P.   Clément Marot: an annotated bibliography, 1983

41. Whinnom, K.   The Spanish Sentimental Romance, 1440-1550, 1983

42. Kennedy, A.J.   Christine de Pizan: a bibliographical guide, 1984

43. Tremewan, P.   Prévost: an analytic bibliography of criticism to 1981, 1984